Roger Scruton (1944–2020) was a man of letters whose many books have been widely translated. His views often ran contrary to what he saw as dominant liberal-left political and academic opinion. He became a Fellow of the Royal Society of Literature in 2003 and of the British Academy in 2008. In 2016 he was knighted for services to 'philosophy, teaching and public education'. In 2018 he was appointed Chair of the Government's Building Better, Building Beautiful Commission tasked with reforming planning law to make beauty an essential consideration.

An annual Scrutopia Summer School devoted to philosophy and conservation continues to run from his home Sunday Hill Farm in Wiltshire. The Roger Scruton Legacy Foundation, founded by one of Scruton's philosophy students, seeks to establish his legacy through supporting the conservation, care, and continuation of humane wisdom and culture from the western tradition. For an active programme of events and reading groups visit www.scruton.org

Douglas Murray is a journalist and bestselling author of six books, including *The Strange Death of Europe* and *The Madness of Crowds*, which was chosen as 'book of the year' by *The Times* and *The Sunday Times*. He is associate editor of *The Spectator* and is a regular contributor to numerous publications including *The Telegraph*, *The Times*, *The Mail on Sunday* and *National Review*. A prolific debater, Murray has appeared on most of the top political debate programmes, including the BBC's *Newsnight*, *Daily Politics*, and *Question Time*.

Notting Hill Editions is an independent British publisher. The company was founded by Tom Kremer (1930–2017), champion of innovation and the man responsible for popularising the Rubik's Cube.

After a successful business career in toy invention Tom decided, at the age of eighty, to fulfil his passion for literature. In a fast-moving digital world Tom's aim was to revive the art of the essay, and to create exceptionally beautiful books that would be lingered over and cherished.

Hailed as 'the shape of things to come', the family-run press brings to print the most surprising thinkers of past and present. In an era of information-overload, these collectible pocket-size books distil ideas that linger in the mind.

CONFESSIONS OF A HERETIC

Roger Scruton

–

Introduced by
Douglas Murray

 Notting Hill Editions

First published in 2016. This edition published in 2021
by Notting Hill Editions Ltd
Mirefoot, Kendal, LA8 9AB

Creative Advisor: Dennis PAPHITIS
Series design by FLOK Design, Berlin, Germany
Cover design by Plain Creative, Kendal, UK
Typeset by CB Editions, London
Printed and bound by Memminger MedienCentrum, Memmingen,
Germany

A CIP record for this book
is available from the British Library

ISBN 978-1-912559-34-3
www.nottinghilleditions.com

Contents

Douglas Murray

– Introduction –

'Heretic' might seem like a strong word to describe Roger Scruton. And yet its use in the title of this beautiful volume is correct and the author was right to suggest it. For though there are eras in which the heretics are of the left, during the era in which Roger Scruton lived and worked it was conservative thought that was at odds with the dogmas of the day.

Of course there are a number of oddities about this. Not least is the time frame in which Scruton first came to prominence. He made his name in the 1980s with *The Meaning of Conservatism* (1980) and his weekly column in *The Times*. Students of what must now be regarded as history will note that Conservatives were not absent from power during this period. Yet during this time conservative ideas remained anomalous if not altogether absent. It is true that conservatives argued and won the economic and geo-political struggles of their day. But aside from these areas, conservative ideas were deemed abhorrent precisely because they were assumed to prevail in government. Nowhere did this happen more than in the university system in which Scruton should have been able to make his career but from which he was effectively cast out for his offending views.

Yet it was not solely the dominance of the ideological left in his day that made Scruton a heretic. For most of his life Scruton was also on the outside on his own political side. As a founding member of the Conservative Philosophy Group, and editor of *The Salisbury Review*, he valiantly attempted to make their ideas relevant to the Conservative party. But Conservatives did not appear to have a need of conservative thinkers as surely as left-wing governments had the need for ideological thinkers of their own ilk. In a further layer of complexity, Scruton did not think that Conservatives were wholly wrong to be suspicious of conservative thought. Indeed the necessity of a suspicion of political philosophy as a whole might be said to be one of the deep but unavoidable contradictions that Scruton had to manage throughout his career.

Having found himself outside of the institutions, Scruton ended up going it all but alone in his professional life. Over the course of four decades he managed an often precarious living outside of the institutions. He wrote books, essays and newspaper pieces. He edited magazines and other volumes. In the long run his accretion of intellectual endeavours brought him admirers. But in the short term what they brought most were highly motivated ideological brickbats. Another person might have been embittered by the embattlement and resulting solitude. But as the years went on and Scruton wrote what he needed to write, the range as well as depth of his achievements became increasingly obvious and marked him out even to many of his one-time opponents.

After all, while other people might have been able to write one of his books, who else could have written them all? Who could have written volumes not just on music but also on architecture, politics and aesthetics? Who could have bothered themselves with the day-to-day fluctuations of a nation's affairs necessary to master a newspaper column while also writing studies on Kant and Spinoza?

Only Scruton could have done all of these things and more. And that is one reason why it was noticeable during the last period of his life – and perhaps even more since his death in 2020 – that he had become so invaluable to a new generation of readers both in Britain and abroad. There are a number of reasons for this, all of which are suggested by the present volume.

The first is that Scruton always went a layer beneath the level at which his contemporaries played. While many people in recent years have written about nationalism and self-determination, few if any have chosen to approach the subject from the very elemental question of the need for belonging. This Scruton does in 'The Need for Nations' among other places, for he knew that while the desire to struggle and fight for things is very strong – especially in the young – the need to reconcile yourself with things, to find a sense of belonging and home in the nation as in the world, is a very deep yearning also. Better than anyone else,

Scruton described how this yearning could find reasonable and respectable form.

Another reason why people gravitated towards Scruton despite – or because – of his heresy was that he took seriously some things which the age had lightly skipped over. For instance he was the most notable figure of any political stripe to take seriously the importance of the built environment. Given that this environment is the only one most people can live in it seems strange that the question of beautiful – or at least not actively ugly – housing should have been so ignored. To the extent that they thought about it at all, most Conservatives seemed to think that this was yet another thing that the market would work out. As our Conservative and Labour-run cities have shown, this hope was wholly misguided. But by focussing his own gaze on the question Scruton ended up provoking even a Conservative government into addressing the question of the places where we live.

And then there was the positive aspect of his vision. Many thinkers and polemicists of the right have been able to deconstruct portions of the left-wing orthodoxies of their day. But it was Scruton's gift to go a stage beyond that. Naturally a part of what he did with his time was criticism. But an equal amount of his time at least was spent doing what so few people do – which was after the deconstruction to go on to construct again, and to rekindle. To put this in practical terms, Scruton showed his readers not just what they should reject, but what they should nurture and love. His writing on music – as here on Strauss's 'Metamorphosen' – is just one gateway into this aspect of his thought.

For he clearly felt that what propelled him might propel his readers also. In one of the most moving essays in this volume ('Effing the Ineffable') he describes how anybody with an open mind and heart will throughout their life encounter 'moments that are saturated with meaning, but whose meaning cannot be put into words. These moments are precious to us. When they occur it is as though, on the winding ill-lit stairway of our life, we suddenly come across a window, through which we catch sight of another and brighter world – a world to which we belong but which we cannot enter.'

Another philosopher might have ignored this aspect of our lives, deeming it either insurmountable or irrelevant to philosophical or other inquiry. Scruton rightly recognised that to do this is to leave unexamined one of the great clues we have to tell us about ourselves and our relationship with the world around us.

Scruton perhaps had a special need to find what these consoling, hopeful signs left for us actually mean. As anybody who knew him can attest, the sense of feeling embattled was very deep in Roger. Throughout his career, right up to the end, he suffered quite extraordinary assaults from people who thought they understood him, but who had barely bothered to scratch his surface: people who had hardly read a word of his books behaved as though they had complete oversight of the whole. Any observer could see that they did not, yet still their scratching affected Roger at some very deep level, constantly fuelling a fear that he was at odds with the world and unacceptable to people who ought to have accepted him. The Knighthood he was awarded in 2016 put some of his feeling of estrangement to rest for a time. But the turbulence was always there.

One of the essays in this volume – 'Dying in Time' – has of course taken on an added layer of significance since its author's death. And it is typical of Scruton that he should have been tempted to struggle with the last of the great questions long before he had to. Just one of the thoughts that occurs from reading it is the extent to which Scruton managed here as elsewhere to live up to his own exacting standards and principles. 'The value of life' he writes 'does not consist in its length but in its depth.' While the length of his own life is over, its depths remain here as in other volumes: ready for new generations of readers to discover and find deep fulfilment in.

– Preface –

This collection of essays arises from a decade of engagement with the public culture of Britain and America. Some have been published in print or on-line; some are appearing here for the first time. I describe them as confessions, since they reveal aspects of my thinking which, if I am to believe the critics, ought to have been kept to myself. I have weeded out material of an academic kind, and have tried to include only those essays that touch on matters of concern to all intelligent people, in the volatile times in which we live.

Scrutopia, Christmas 2015

– Faking It –

'To thine own self be true,' says Shakespeare's Polonius, 'and thou canst be false to no man.' Live in truth, urged Václav Havel. 'Let the lie come into the world,' wrote Solzhenitsyn, 'but not through me.' How seriously should we take these pronouncements, and how do we obey them?

There are two kinds of untruth: lying and faking. The person who is lying says what he does not believe. The person who is faking says what he believes, though only for the time being and for the purpose in hand.

Anyone can lie. It suffices to say something with the intention to deceive. Faking, however, is an achievement. To fake things you have to take people in, yourself included. The liar can pretend to be shocked when his lies are exposed: but his pretence is part of the lie. The fake really *is* shocked when he is exposed, since he had created around himself a community of trust, of which he himself was a member.

In all ages people have lied in order to escape the consequences of their actions, and the first step in moral education is to teach children not to tell fibs. But faking is a cultural phenomenon, more prominent in some periods than in others. There is very little faking in the society described by Homer, for example, or in that described by Chaucer. By the time of Shakespeare, however, poets and playwrights are beginning to take a strong interest in this new human type.

In Shakespeare's *King Lear* the wicked sisters Goneril and Regan belong to a world of fake emotion, persuading themselves and their father that they feel the deepest love, when in fact they are entirely heartless. But they don't really know themselves to be heartless: if they did, they could not behave so brazenly. The tragedy of King Lear begins when the real people – Kent, Cordelia, Edgar, Gloucester – are driven out by the fakes.

The fake is a person who has rebuilt himself, with a view to occupying another social position than the one that would be natural to him. Such is Molière's Tartuffe, the religious imposter who takes control of a household through a display of scheming piety, and who gave his name to the vice that his creator was perhaps the first to pinpoint with total accuracy. Like Shakespeare, Molière perceived that faking goes to the very heart of the person engaged in it. Tartuffe is not simply a hypocrite, who pretends to ideals that he does not believe in. He is a fabricated person, who believes in his own ideals since he is just as illusory as they are.

Tartuffe's faking was a matter of sanctimonious religion. With the decline of religion during the 19th century there came about a new kind of faking. The romantic poets and painters turned their backs

2

on religion and sought salvation through art. They believed in the genius of the artist, endowed with a special capacity to transcend the human condition in creative ways, breaking all the rules in order to achieve a new order of experience. Art became an avenue to the transcendental, the gateway to a higher kind of knowledge.

Originality therefore became the test that distinguishes true from fake art. It is hard to say in general terms what originality consists in, but we have examples enough: Titian, Beethoven, Goethe, Baudelaire. But those examples teach us that originality is hard: it cannot be snatched from the air, even if there are those natural prodigies like Rimbaud and Mozart who seem to do just that. Originality requires learning, hard work, the mastery of a medium and – most of all – the refined sensibility and openness to experience that have suffering and solitude as their normal cost.

To gain the status of an original artist is therefore not easy. But in a society where art is revered as the highest cultural achievement, the rewards are enormous. Hence there is a motive to fake it. Artists and critics get together in order to take themselves in, the artists posing as the originators of astonishing breakthroughs, the critics posing as the penetrating judges of the true avant-garde.

In this way Duchamp's famous urinal became a kind of paradigm for modern artists. This is how it is done, the critics said. Take an idea, put it on display, call it art and brazen it out. The trick was repeated with Andy Warhol's Brillo boxes, and then later with the pickled sharks and cows of Damien Hirst. In each case the critics have gathered like clucking hens around the new and inscrutable egg, and the fake is projected to the public with all the apparatus required for its acceptance as the real thing. So powerful is the impetus towards the collective fake that it is now rare to be a finalist for the Turner Prize without producing some object or event that shows itself to be art only because nobody would conceivably think it to be so until the critics have said that it is.

Original gestures of the kind introduced by Duchamp cannot really be repeated – like jokes they can be made only once. Hence the cult of originality very quickly leads to repetition. The habit of faking becomes so deeply engrained that no judgement is certain, except the judgement that this before us is the 'real thing' and not a fake at all, which in turn is a fake judgement. All that we know, in the end, is that anything is art, because nothing is.

It is worth asking ourselves why the cult of fake originality has such a powerful appeal to our cultural institutions, so that no museum or art gallery, and no publicly funded concert hall, can really afford not to take it seriously. The early modernists – Stravinsky and Schoenberg in music, Eliot and Pound in poetry, Matisse in painting and Loos in architecture – were united in the belief that popular taste had become corrupted, that sentimentality, banality and kitsch had invaded the various spheres of art and eclipsed their messages. Tonal harmonies had been corrupted by popular music, figurative painting had been trumped by photography; rhyme and meter had become the stuff of Christmas cards, and the stories had been too often told. Everything out there, in the world of naive and unthinking people, was kitsch.

Modernism was the attempt to rescue the sincere, the truthful, the arduously achieved, from the plague of fake emotion. No one can doubt that the early modernists succeeded in this enterprise, endowing us with works of art that keep the human spirit alive in the new circumstances of modernity, and which establish continuity with the great traditions of our culture. But modernism gave way to routines of fakery: the arduous task of maintaining the tradition proved less attractive than the cheap ways of rejecting it. Instead of Picasso's lifelong study, to present the modern woman's face in a modern idiom, you could just do what Duchamp did, and paint a moustache on the Mona Lisa.

The interesting fact, however, is that the habit of faking it has arisen from the fear of fakes. Modernist art was a reaction against fake emotion, and the comforting clichés of popular culture. The intention was to sweep away the pseudo-art that cushions us with sentimental lies and to put reality, the reality of modern life, with which real art alone can come to terms, in the place of it. Hence for a long time now it has been assumed that there can be no authentic creation in the sphere of high art which is not in some way a 'challenge' to the complacencies of our public culture. Art must give offence, stepping out of the future fully armed against the bourgeois taste for the conforming and the comfortable, which are simply other names for kitsch and cliché. But the result of this is that offence becomes a cliché. If the public has become so immune to shock that only a dead shark in formaldehyde will awaken a brief spasm of outrage, then the artist must produce a dead shark in formaldehyde – this, at least, is an authentic gesture.

There therefore grew around the modernists a class of critics and impresarios, who offered to explain just why it is not a waste of your time to stare at a pile of bricks, to sit quietly through ten minutes of excruci-ating noise, or to study a crucifix pickled in urine. The experts began to promote the incomprehensible and the outrageous as a matter of course, lest the public should regard its services as redundant. To convince themselves that they are true progressives, who ride in the vanguard of history, the new impresarios surround themselves with others of their kind, promoting them to all committees that are relevant to their status, and expecting to be promoted in their turn. Thus arose the modernist establishment – the self-contained circle of critics who form the backbone of our official and semi-official cultural institutions and who trade in 'originality', 'transgression' and 'breaking new paths'.

Those are the routine terms issued by the Arts Council bureaucrats and the museum establishment, whenever they want to spend public money on something that they would never dream of having in their living room. But these terms are clichés, as are the things they are used to praise. Hence the flight from cliché ends in cliché, and the attempt to be genuine ends in fake.

In the attacks on the old ways of doing things, one word in particular came into currency. That word was 'kitsch'. Once introduced the word stuck. Whatever you do, it mustn't be kitsch. This became the first precept of the modernist artist in every medium. In a famous essay published in 1939, the American critic Clement Greenberg told his readers that there are only two possibilities available to the artist now. Either you belong to the avant-garde, challenging the old ways of figurative painting; or you produce kitsch. And the fear of kitsch is one reason for the compulsory offensiveness of so much art produced today. It doesn't matter that your work is obscene, shocking, disturbing – as long as it isn't kitsch.

Nobody quite knows where the word 'kitsch' came from, though it was current in Germany and Austria at the end of the 19th century. Nobody knows quite how to define the word either. But we all recognise kitsch when we come across it. The Barbie doll; Walt Disney's Bambi; Santa Claus in the supermarket; Bing Crosby singing 'White Christmas'; pictures of poodles with ribbons in their hair. At Christmas we are surrounded by kitsch – worn out clichés, which have lost their innocence without achieving wisdom. Children who believe in Santa Claus invest real emotions in a fiction. We who have ceased to believe have only fake emotions to offer. But the faking is pleasant; it feels good to pretend; and when we all join in it is almost as though we were not pretending at all.

The Czech novelist Milan Kundera made a famous observation. 'Kitsch,' he wrote, 'causes two tears to flow in quick succession. The first tear says: How nice to see children running on the grass! The second tear says: how nice to be moved, together with all mankind, by children running on the grass!' Kitsch, in other words, is not about the thing observed but about the observer. It does not invite you to feel moved by the doll you are dressing so tenderly, but by yourself dressing the doll. All sentimentality is like this: it redirects emotion from the object to the subject, so as to create a fantasy of emotion without the real cost of feeling it. The kitsch object encourages you to think 'look at me feeling this; how nice I am and how lovable'. That is why Oscar Wilde, referring to one of Dickens's most sickly death-scenes, said that 'a man must have a heart of stone not to laugh at the death of Little Nell'.

And that, briefly, is why the modernists had such a horror of kitsch. Art, they believed, had, during the course of the 19th century, lost the ability to distinguish precise and real emotion from its vague and self-satisfied substitute. In figurative painting, in tonal music, in the cliché-ridden poems of heroic love and mythic glory, we find the same disease – the artist is not exploring the human heart but creating a puffed-up substitute, and then putting it on sale.

Of course, you can use the old styles; but you cannot seriously mean them. And if you use them nevertheless, the result will be kitsch – standard, cut-price goods, produced without effort and consumed without thought. Figurative painting becomes the stuff of Christmas cards, music becomes spineless and sentimental, and literature collapses into cliché. Kitsch is fake art, expressing fake emotions, whose purpose is to deceive the consumer into thinking he feels something deep and serious, when in fact he feels nothing at all.

However, to avoid kitsch is not so easy as it looks. You could try being outrageously avant-garde, doing something that no one would have thought of doing and calling it art; perhaps trampling on some cherished ideal or religious feeling. But this way also leads to fakes – fake originality, fake significance, and a new kind of cliché, as in so much Young British Art. You can pose as a modernist, but that won't necessarily lead you to achieve what Eliot, Schoenberg or Matisse achieved, which is to touch the modern heart in its deepest regions. Modernism is difficult; it requires competence in an artistic tradition, and the art of departing from tradition in order to say something new.

This is one reason for the emergence of a wholly new artistic enterprise, which I call 'pre-emptive kitsch'. Modernist severity is both difficult and unpopular; so artists began not to shun kitsch but to embrace it, in the manner of Andy Warhol, Allen Jones and Jeff Koons. The worst thing is to be unwittingly guilty of producing kitsch; far better to produce kitsch deliberately, for then it is not kitsch at all but a kind of sophisticated parody. Pre-emptive kitsch sets quotation marks around actual kitsch, and hopes thereby to save its artistic credentials. Take a porcelain statue of Michael Jackson cuddling his pet chimpanzee Bubbles, add cheesy colours and a layer of varnish; set the figures up in the posture of a Madonna and child; endow them with soppy expressions as though challenging the spectator to vomit, and the result is such kitsch that it cannot possibly be kitsch. Jeff Koons must mean something else, we think, something deep and serious that we have missed. Perhaps this work of art is really a comment on kitsch, so that by being explicitly kitsch it becomes meta-kitsch, so to speak.

Or take Allen Jones, whose art consists of female look-alikes contorted into furniture, dolls with their sexual parts made explicit by underwear, vulgar and childishly nasty visions of the human female, the whole as frothy with fake sentiment as any simpering fashion model. Again the result is such obvious kitsch that it cannot be kitsch. The artist must be telling us something about ourselves – about our desires and lusts – and forcing us to confront the fact that we like kitsch, while he pours scorn on kitsch by laying it on with a trowel. In place of our imagined ideals in gilded frames, he offers real junk in quotation marks.

Pre-emptive kitsch is the first link in a chain. The artist pretends to take himself seriously, the critics pretend to judge his product and the modernist establishment pretends to promote it. At the end of all this pretence, someone who cannot perceive the difference between the real thing and the fake decides that he should buy it. Only at this point does the chain of pretence come to an end, and the real value of this kind of art reveal itself – namely its money value. Even at this point, however, the pretence is important. The purchaser must still believe that what he buys is real art, and therefore intrinsically valuable, a bargain at any price. Otherwise the price would reflect the obvious fact that anybody – even the purchaser – could have faked such a product. The essence of fakes is that they are not really themselves, but substitutes for themselves. Like objects seen in parallel mirrors they repeat themselves ad infinitum, and at each repetition the price goes up a notch, to the point where a balloon dog by Jeff Koons, which every child could conceive and many could manufacture, fetches the highest price ever paid for a work by a living artist – except, of course, that he isn't one.

Fake originality, fake emotion and the fake expertise of the critics – these are all around us and in such abundance that we hardly know where to look for the real thing. Or perhaps there is no real thing? Perhaps the world of art is just one vast pretence, in which we all take part since, after all, there is no real cost to it, except to those like Charles Saatchi, rich enough to splash out on junk? Perhaps anything is art if someone says that it is. Perhaps there is no such thing as a qualified judge. 'It's all a matter of taste,' they say. And that's about as far as thinking goes. But is there nothing to be said in reply? Do we have no way of distinguishing true from false art, or saying why art matters and how? I shall make a few positive suggestions.

First, however, we must ignore the factors that distort our judgment. Paintings and sculptures can be owned, bought and sold. Hence there is a vast market in them, and whether or not they have a value, they certainly have a price. Oscar Wilde defined the cynic as the one who knows the price of everything, and the value of nothing. And the art market is inevitably run by cynics. Utter trash accumulates in our museums largely because it has a price tag. You cannot own a symphony or a novel in the way you can own a Damien Hirst. As a result there are far fewer fake symphonies or fake novels than there are fake works of visual art.

Things are distorted too by the channels of official patronage. The Arts Council exists to subsidise those artists, writers and musicians whose work is important. But how do bureaucrats decide that something is important? The culture tells them that a work is important if it is original, and the proof that a work is original is that the public doesn't like it. Besides, if the public *did* like it, why would it need a subsidy? Official patronage therefore inevitably favours works that are arcane, excruciating or meaningless over those that have real and lasting appeal.

So what is the source of that appeal, and how do we judge that a work of art possesses it? Three words summarise my answer: 'beauty', 'form' and 'redemption'.

For many artists and critics beauty is a discredited idea. It denotes the saccharine sylvan scenes and cheesy melodies that appealed to Granny. The modernist message, that art must show life as it is, suggests to many people that, if you aim for beauty, you will end up with kitsch. This is a mistake, however. Kitsch tells you how nice you are: it offers easy feelings on the cheap. Beauty tells you to stop thinking about yourself, and to wake up to the world of others. It says, look at this, listen to this, study this – for here is something more important than you. Kitsch is a means to cheap emotion; beauty is an end in itself. We reach beauty through setting our interests aside and letting the world *dawn* on us. There are many ways of doing this, but art is undeniably the most important, since it presents us with the image of human life – our own life and all that life means to us – and asks us to look on it directly, not for what we can take from it but for what we can give to it. Through beauty art cleans the world of our self-obsession.

Our human need for beauty is not something that

we could lack and still be fulfilled as people. It is a need arising from our moral nature. We can wander through this world, alienated, resentful, full of suspicion and distrust. Or we can find our home here, coming to rest in harmony with others and with ourselves. And the experience of beauty guides us along this second path: it tells us that we *are* at home in the world, that the world is already ordered in our perceptions as a place fit for the lives of beings like us. That is what we see in Corot's landscapes, Cézanne's apples, or Van Gogh's unlaced boots.

The true work of art is not beautiful in the way an animal, a flower or a stretch of countryside is beautiful. It is a consciously created thing, in which the human need for form triumphs over the randomness of objects. Our lives are fragmented and distracted: things start up in our feelings without finding their completion. Very little is revealed to us in such a way that its significance can be fully understood. In art, however, we create a realm of the imagination, in which each beginning finds its end, and each fragment is part of a meaningful whole. The subject of a Bach fugue seems to develop of its own accord, filling musical space and moving logically towards closure. But it is not an exercise in mathematics. Every theme in Bach is pregnant with emotion, moving with the rhythm of the listener's inner life. Bach is taking you into an imagined space, and presenting you, in that space, with the image of your own fulfilment. Likewise Rembrandt will take the flesh tints on an ageing face and show how each one captures something of the life within, so that the formal harmony of the colours conveys the completeness and unity of the person. In Rembrandt we see integrated character in a disintegrating body. And we are moved to reverence.

Formal perfection cannot be achieved without knowledge, discipline and attention to detail. People are slowly beginning to understand this. The illusion that art flows out of us, and that the only purpose of an art school is to teach us how to open the taps, is no longer believable. Gone are the days when you can make a stir by wrapping a building in polystyrene like Christo or sitting in silence at a piano for 4 minutes and 33 seconds like John Cage. To be really modern, you must create works of art that take modern life, in all its disconnectedness, and bring it to fullness and resolution, as Philip Larkin did in his great poem 'The Whitsun Weddings'. It is fine for a composer to lard his pieces with dissonant sounds and cluster chords like Harrison Birtwistle; but if he knows nothing of harmony and counterpoint the result will be random noise, not music. It is fine for a painter to splash paint around like Jackson Pollock, but the real knowledge of colour comes through studying the natural world, and finding our own emotions mirrored in the secret tints of things, as Cézanne found peace and comfort in a dish of apples.

If we look at the true apostles of beauty in our

time – I think of composers like Henri Dutilleux and James MacMillan, of painters like David Inshaw and John Wonnacott, of poets like Ruth Padel and Charles Tomlinson, of prose writers like Italo Calvino and Georges Perec – we are immediately struck by the immense hard work, the studious isolation, and the attention to detail which have characterised their craft. In art beauty has to be *won*, and the work is harder, as the surrounding idiocy grows. In the face of sorrow, imperfection and the fleetingness of our affections and joys, we ask ourselves 'why?'. We need reassurance. We look to art for the proof that life in this world is meaningful and that suffering is not the pointless thing that it so often appears to be, but the necessary part of a larger and redeeming whole. Tragedies show us the triumph of dignity over destruction and compassion over despair. In a way that will always be mysterious, they endow suffering with a formal completion and thereby restore the moral equilibrium. The tragic hero is completed through his fate; his death is a sacrifice, and this sacrifice renews the world.

Tragedy reminds us that beauty is a redemptive presence in our lives: it is the face of love, shining in the midst of desolation. We should not be surprised that many of the most beautiful works of modern art have emerged in reaction to hatred and cruelty. The poems of Akhmatova, the writings of Pasternak, the music of Shostakovitch – such works shone a light in the totalitarian darkness, and showed love in the midst of destruction. Something similar could be said of Eliot's *Four Quartets,* of Britten's *War Requiem*, of Matisse's chapel at Vence.

Modernism arose because artists, writers and musicians held on to the vision of beauty, as a redemptive presence in our lives. And that is the difference between the real work of art and the fake. Real art is a work of love; fake art is a work of deception.

2

– Loving Animals –

I live on a pasture farm, in a part of England where a thin topsoil covers a sub-soil of clay. You can grow grass on this topsoil; but you cannot plough it without turning up the clay, on which nothing grows; the only human use for the land, therefore, is to support things that live on grass or its by-products. That means cows, sheep, pigs, chickens by way of domestic animals, game birds by way of wildlife, and horses for riding. By far the most profitable of these animals, from the point of view of our local farming economy, are the horses, which bring people who earn *real* money into the countryside, and encourage them to turn that money into grass. Those who are trying to turn grass into money have a much harder time of it. Still, all in all, I see our little patch of farmland as an example of good-natured animal husbandry. All our animals live in an environment to which they are adapted, enjoy basic freedoms, and are saved by our intervention from the lingering misery of old age and disease, or from a long-drawn-out death from physical injury. This is true, for the most part, of the wildlife too. The game birds are either shot or eaten by the fox, the rats, field-mice, voles and other rodents are taken by the buzzards and hawks, and the fish are quickly swallowed by the visiting heron. Death from old age, disease or injury is rare, and we do what we can to help our wild animals through the winter, with scraps from the kitchen for the carnivores and corn and nuts for the birds.

Of course there is much room for improvement, and there are aspects of our management that disturb me. In particular it worries me that our natural affections favour some animals over others. Thus we go out of our way to ensure that the predators get through the hard days of winter, but do little or nothing for the mice and voles, and do what we can to exterminate the rats. Of course, we don't poison the rats, since that would be to poison the owls, buzzards and foxes that eat their remains. But we interfere in the natural order, and could not envisage life on the farm if we did not do so. Hares are welcome, rabbits less so; stoats and weasels enjoy our protection, crows and magpies don't dare to come within range. So far I have not met any country person who does not make choices of the kind that we make, and when I read of 'wildlife sanctuaries' I wonder how far their wardens are prepared to go, by way of managing those species which, if left to themselves, will turn a viable habitat into a desert – grey squirrels, for instance, Canada geese, cormorants.

Although I worry about our meddling in the order that surrounds us, I take comfort from the fact that species that were never seen on the farm when I bought it twenty years ago are now re-establishing their presence there: bullfinches, wagtails, kestrels, kitty hawks, fallow deer, stoats and grass-snakes. We have many kinds of bee, and the ponds abound in frogs, toads and dragonflies. But we also have neighbours, and by far the greatest threat to the animals that live on our land comes from that source. I don't refer to the farming neighbours, who maintain the ecological balance in much the way that we do. I refer to the incomers, those who have moved to the country in order to enjoy the tranquillity that is the by-product of other peoples' farming, and who come with their own menagerie of animals – much loved animals, who have enjoyed all the creature comforts that the town can provide. It is the dogs and cats of these people that do most to upset the fragile order that we have tried to maintain, and I cannot help drawing some conclusions about the distinction between the right and the wrong ways of loving them.

One neighbour has a dog which she walks along the public bridleway, leaving it free to run in the hedgerows and out into the fields. This dog does what dogs do: it sniffs for quarry and, when it finds something, gives chase. In the winter, when birds are hidden under leaves, conserving their energy as best they can, they cannot easily survive being chased every day. The same is true of hares, rabbits and voles. Of course our neighbour is adamant that her dog would not dream of killing the things he chases – he is only doing what his nature requires. The same is true, of course, of the pheasant, the stoat or the rabbit that he is chasing. The difference is that the dog goes home to a warm house and a supper consisting largely of other animals which have been tortured into a tin, while its quarry goes hungry, trying to recover from the shock and weakened for its next encounter.

Another neighbour has a pair of cats – attractive animals, which know how to simulate affection towards their human owners, while policing all around them with the invincible insolence of a dominant species. Both dogs and cats are predators; but dogs can be trained not to kill; they can be trained to focus their hunting instincts on a particular species, or they can be bred to focus the very same instincts on some other and more humanly useful pursuit, such as herding sheep or retrieving game birds. Not so cats. Everything in their nature tends towards the single goal of killing, and although they can be pampered into relinquishing this goal, they are by that same process pampered into relinquishing their nature. A true cat wants out, and when out he wants death. The distinctions between fair and unfair game, between vermin and protected species, between friend and foe – all such distinctions have no significance for a cat, which sets off from the house in search of songbirds, field mice, shrews and other harmless and necessary creatures with no thought for anything save the taste in his mouth of their blood. One estimate puts at 180 million the number of wild birds and mammals lost to cats each year in Britain.[1] The domestic cat is, without exception, the most devastating of all the alien species that have been brought onto our island, and the worst of it is that, thanks to the sentimentality of the British animal lover, it is a crime to shoot them.

Love has many forms, and there is no reason to suppose that my love of farm animals and wildlife is in any way superior, as an emotion, to the love of our neighbours for their dogs and cats. But two questions should be asked of every love: does it benefit the object, and does it benefit the subject? Whether or not we agree with Wilde's bathetic line that 'Each man kills the thing he loves', it is certainly true that there are loves that destroy their object, for the reasons given by Blake:

> Love seeketh only self to please
> To bind another to its delight,
> Joys in another's loss of ease
> And builds a Hell in Heav'n's despite.

There are loves that enslave, stifle, exploit and abuse. And there again there are loves that corrupt the subject, giving him a false and flattering view of himself, and a comforting picture of his own cost-free lovableness. Love is not good in itself; it is good when part of virtue, bad when part of vice. In which case we should follow Aristotle, and say that it is not as such good to love, but good to love the right object, on the right occasion and to the right degree.[2] Learning how and what to love is part of growing up, and love, like other emotions, must be disciplined if it is not to collapse into sentimentality on the one hand, or domination on the other.

There is much literature that takes the love between humans and animals as its subject, and we are none of us short of examples, with which to explore what might be good, and what bad, in such a cross-species affection. I am as susceptible to the love of pets as anyone, and still remember my childhood dog, a repulsive creature entirely deficient in canine virtues, as an object of deep and need-filled emotion. When my horse Barney, whom I loved, died beneath me while hunting, I was quite stricken for a while, until setting eyes on Barney's successor. Cats have always taken a shine to me, purring and kneading in my lap with no knowledge of the contempt in which I hold their species. Still, none of this should impede me from asking the question when, and how, it is right to love an animal.

The first point to make is that love for animals is only exceptionally love for an individual animal. I love the animals on our farm but few of them are objects of an individual love: it is the presence of bullfinches, not of any particular bullfinch, that delights me, and for which I work as best I can. Of course I am concerned when I come cross a bird or a mammal in distress, and will go out of my way to help it: but this is not love, only ordinary kindness. With the horses it is different, since I stand to them in another relation, knowing their individual traits and foibles, and riding them, often in hair-raising circumstances in which we depend on each other for safety and maybe even survival. A special bond grows from such circumstances – the bond that caused Alexander the Great to mourn the brave Bucephalus and to build a city in his honour. However, it is unclear that horses respond to their riders as *individuals*, or that they are capable of feeling the kind of affection, either for us or for each other, that we feel for them. They distinguish a good place from a bad one; they recognise and relate to their stable mates; they know what kind of treatment to expect from which of the two-legged creatures that come to care for them. But their affections are weak, unfocused and easily transferred. Barney, for me, had some of the qualities of Bucephalus: bold, eager to be first in the field, and obedient in the face of danger. And that was the ground of my affection: not that he regarded me with any favour or made a place for me in his life as I made a place for him in mine.

Now it seems to me that there are bad ways of loving a horse: ways that are bad for the horse, and also bad for the one who loves him. A love that regards the horse as a play-thing, whose purpose is to satisfy the whims of a rider, to be an object of cuddling and caressing of a kind that the horse himself can neither reciprocate nor understand – such a love is a way of disregarding the horse. It is also in its own way corrupt. A person who lavishes this kind of affection on a horse is either deceiving himself or else taking pleasure in a fantasy affection, treating the horse as a means to his own emotion, which has become the real focus of his concern. The horse has become the object of a self-regarding love, a love without true care for the thing that occasions it. Such a love takes no true note of the horse, and is quite compatible with a ruthless neglect of the animal, when it loses (as it will) its superficial attractions. Horses treated in this way are frequently discarded, like the dolls of children. And it is indeed the case of the doll that provides, for the philosophy of love, the most poignant instance of error. Children practise affection with their dolls: it is their way of developing in themselves the expressions, habits and gestures that will elicit protection and love from those around them. But we expect them, for this reason, to grow out of dolls and into proper love – love that bears a cost for the one who feels it, which puts the self in the hands of another, and which forms the foundation of a reciprocal bond of care.

Each species is different, and when it comes to dogs there is no doubt, not only that dogs reciprocate the affection of their masters, but also that they become attached to their masters as *individuals*, in a way that renders the master irreplaceable in their affections – so much so that the grief of a dog may strike us as desolate beyond anything that we, who have access even in extremity to consolation, could really feel. The focused devotion of a dog is – when it occurs (and not all dogs are capable of it) – one of the most moving of all the gifts that we receive from animals, all the more moving for not being truly a gift but rather a need.[3] It seems to me that the recipient of such a love is under a duty to the creature that offers it, and that this creates a quite special ground for love that we must take into account. The owner of a loving dog has a duty of care beyond that of the owner of a horse. To neglect or abandon such a dog is to betray a trust that creates an objective obligation, and an obligation towards an individual. Hence my neighbour is right to think that her obligation to her dog takes precedence over my duty to care for the wildlife whose welfare he is compromising. She occupies one pole of a relation of trust, and it would be a moral deficiency in her to assume the right to enjoy her dog's unswerving affection while denying him what she can easily provide by way of a reward for it. Hence I don't judge her adversely for her irritating dog or her equally irritating love for it: the fault is mine, like the fault of being upset by the selfishness of families, as they strive to secure the best seats on a train. Each of us has a sphere of love, and he is bound to the others who inhabit it.

That said, however, we should still make a distinction between the right way and the wrong way to love a dog. Dogs are individuals, in the way that all animals are individuals. But they have, if it can be so expressed, a higher degree of individuality than birds, certainly a higher degree of individuality than insects. By this I mean that their wellbeing is more bound up with their specific nature and circumstances, with their affections and their character, than is the wellbeing of members of other species. A bird relates to its surroundings as a member of its species, but not as one who has created for itself an individual network of expectations and fears. The loving dog is dependent on individual people, and knows that he is so dependent. He responds to his surroundings in ways that distinguish individuals within it, and recognises demands that are addressed specifically to him, and to which he must respond. His emotions, simple though they are, are *learned* responses, which bear the imprint of a history of mutual dealings.

In this way it is possible to read into the behaviour of a dog something of the inter-personal responses that we know from human affection. The dog is not a person, but he is like a person in incorporating into himself the distinguishing features of his experience, coming to be the particular dog that he is through being related to the particular others in his surroundings. But why do I say he is not a person? The reason, briefly, is this. Persons are individuals too; but their individuality is situated on another metaphysical plane from that of the animals, even that of the animals who love them, and love them as individuals. Persons identify themselves in the first person, know themselves as

'I', and make free choices based on these acts of identification. They are sovereign over their world, and the distinction between self and other, mine and not-mine, deciding and not deciding, penetrates all their thinking and acting.

The dog who looks into the eyes of his master is not judging, not reminding the master of his responsibilities or putting himself on display as another individual with rights and freedoms of his own. He is simply appealing as he might to a mate or a fellow member of the pack, in the hope that his need will be answered. There is not, in any of this, the 'I' to 'I' encounter that distinguishes persons among all other things in nature and which, indeed, for Kant, is a sign that they are not really part of nature at all. Although I relate to my dog as an individual, it is from a plane of individuality to which he can never ascend. Ideas of responsibility, duty, right and freedom, which govern my intentions, have no place in his thinking. For him I am another animal – a very special animal, certainly, but nevertheless one that exists on the same plane as himself, and whose motives he will never comprehend, except in terms of the kind of unquestioning unity of being that is the sum of canine affection.

Now it seems to me that the right way to love a dog is to love him not as a person, but as a creature that has been raised to the edge of personhood, so as to look into a place that is opaque to him but from which emerge signals that he understands in another way than we who send them. If we base our love for our dog on the premise that he, like us, is a person, then we damage both him and ourselves. We damage him by making demands that no animal can fully understand – holding him to account in ways that make no sense to him. We will feel bound to keep him alive, as we keep each other alive, for the sake of a relation that, being personal, is also eternal. It seems to me that a person loves his dog wrongly when he does not have him put down when decay is irreversible. But it is not so much the damage done to the dog that matters: it is the damage done to the person. The love of a dog is in an important sense cost-free. The greatest criminal can enjoy it. No dog demands virtue or honour of his master, and all dogs will leap to their master's defence, even when it is the forces of good that are coming to arrest him. Dogs do not judge, and their love is unconditional only because it has no conception of conditions. From a dog, therefore, we can enjoy the kind of endorsement that requires no moral labour to earn it. And this is what we see all around us: the dwindling of human affection, which is always conditional and always dependent on moral work, and its replacement by the cost-free love of pets.

Such a love wants to have it both ways: to preserve the pre-lapsarian innocence of its object, while believing the object capable nevertheless of moral judgement. The dog is a dumb animal, and therefore incapable of wrongdoing; but for that very reason he is seen as right in all his judgements, bestowing his affection on worthy objects, and endorsing his master through his love. This is the root cause of the sentimentalisation of animal life that makes a film like *Bambi* so poisonous – leading people to 'dollify' animals, while believing the animals to be 'in the right' and always endowed with the moral advantage. But you cannot have it both ways: either animals are outside the sphere of moral judgement, or they are not. If they are outside it, then their behaviour cannot be taken as proof of their 'innocence'. If they are inside it, then they may sometimes be guilty and deserving of blame.

Human love is of many kinds. In its highest form, it comes as a gift, freely bestowed on another person along with the offer of support. But such love does not come without cost. There is a cost to the subject, and a cost to the object. Love can be betrayed by its object, when he shows himself to be unworthy to receive it, and incapable of returning it. And to undergo this experience is one of the greatest of human griefs. But love for that very reason imposes a cost on its object, who must live up to the trust bestowed on him, and do his best to deserve the gift. Love is a moral challenge that we do not always meet, and in the effort to meet it we study to improve ourselves and to live as we should. It is for this reason that we are suspicious of loveless people – people who do not offer love and who therefore, in the normal run of things, do not receive it. It is not simply that they are outside the fold of human affection. It is that they are cut off from the principal spur to human goodness, which is the desire to live up to the demands of a person who matters to them more than they matter themselves.

Clearly, if we conceive human love in that way, we can see that we all have a strong motive to avoid it: we do not benefit by avoiding it, and it is always a mistake to try, as we know from the tragedy of *King Lear.*[4] Nevertheless, life is simpler without inter-personal love, since it can be lived at a lower level, beneath the glare of moral judgement. And that is the *bad* reason for lavishing too much feeling on a pet. Devoted animals provide an escape-route from human affection, and so make that affection superfluous. Of course, people can find themselves so beaten down by life, so deprived of human love that, through no fault of their own, they devote themselves to the care of an animal, by way of keeping the lamp of affection alive. Such is Flaubert's *Coeur simple*, whose devotion to her parrot was in no way a moral failing. But that kind of devotion, which is the residue of genuine moral feeling, is a virtue in the one who displays it, and has little in common with the Bambyism that is now growing all around us, and which seeks to rewrite our relations with other animals in the language of rights.

I have argued against the idea of animal rights elsewhere.[5] My argument stems, not from a disrespect for animals, but from a respect for moral reasoning, and for the concepts – right, duty, obligation, virtue –

which it employs and which depend at every point on the distinctive features of self-consciousness. But perhaps the greatest damage done by the idea of animal rights is the damage to animals themselves. Elevated in this way to the plane of moral consciousness, they find themselves unable to respond to the distinctions that morality requires. They do not distinguish right from wrong; they cannot recognise the call of duty or the binding obligations of the moral law. And because of this we judge them purely in terms of their ability to share our domestic ambience, to profit from our affection, and from time to time to reciprocate it in their own mute and dependent way. And it is precisely this that engenders our unscrupulous favouritism – the favouritism that has made it a crime in my country to shoot a cat, however destructive its behaviour, but a praiseworthy action to poison a mouse, and thereby to infect the food-chain on which so many animals depend.

It is not that we should withdraw our love from our favourite animals: to the extent that they depend on that love to that extent we should continue to provide it. But we must recognise that by loving them as *individuals* we threaten the animals who cannot easily be loved in any such way. Loving our dogs and cats we put a strain upon the natural order that is felt most grievously by the birds and beasts of the field. And even if those creatures have no rights, this does not cancel the fact that we have duties towards them – duties that become everyday more serious and demanding, as we humans expand to take over the habitats that we confiscate without scruple and enjoy without remorse. And our lack of scruple is only amplified by the sentimental attitudes that are nurtured by the love of pets, and which inculcate in us the desire for easy-going, cost-free and self-congratulatory affections, and which thereby undermine the human virtue on which the rest of nature most depends.

3

– Governing Rightly –

I n his first Inaugural Address, President Reagan announced that 'government is not the solution to our problem; government is the problem', and his remark struck a chord in the hearts of his conservative supporters. American conservatives, called upon to define their position, reiterate the message that there is 'too much government'. The seemingly unstoppable expansion of regulations, the increasing control over what happens in the work-place, in the public square and even in the family, the constant manufacture of new crimes and misdemeanours, aimed at controlling how we associate and with whom, the attempts to limit first and second-amendment rights – these developments are viewed by many conservatives with alarm. They seem to be taking America in a new direction, away from the free association of self-governing individuals envisaged by the Founders, towards a society of obedient dependents, who exchange their freedom and their responsibilities for a perpetual lien on the public purse. And you only have to look at Europe to see the result.

The European countries are governed by a political class that can escape from accountability behind the closed doors of the European institutions. Those institutions deliver an unending flow of laws and regulations covering all aspects of life, from the hours of work to the rights of sexual minorities. Everywhere in the European Union a regime of political correctness makes it difficult either to maintain, or to live by, precepts that violate the state-imposed orthodoxies. Non-discrimination laws force many religious people to go against the teachings of their faith – in the matters of homosexuality, public preaching and the display of religious symbols. Activists in the European Parliament seek to impose on all states of the Union, regardless of culture, faith or sovereignty, an unqualified right to abortion, together with forms of 'sex education' calculated to prepare young people as commodities in the sexual market, rather than as responsible adults seeking commitment and love.[1]

A kind of hysteria of repudiation rages in European opinion-forming circles, picking one by one on the old and settled customs of a two-thousand-year-old civilisation, and forbidding them or distorting them into some barely recognisable caricature. And all this goes with a gradual transfer of economic life from private enterprise to central government, so that in France and Italy more than half of citizens are net recipients of income from the state while small businesses struggle to comply with a regime of regulations that seems designed on purpose to suppress them.

Many of those developments are being replicated

in America. The welfare state has expanded beyond the limits envisaged in the New Deal, and the Supreme Court is now increasingly used to impose the morality of a liberal elite on the American people, whether they like it or not. These developments add to the sense among conservatives that government is taking over. America, they fear, is rapidly surrendering the rights and freedoms of its citizens in exchange for the false security of an all-controlling state. Those tasks that only governments can perform – defence of the realm, the maintenance of law and order, the repair of infrastructure and the coordination of relief in emergencies – are forced to compete for their budgets with activities that free citizens, left to themselves, might have managed far more efficiently through the associations of volunteers, backed up where necessary by private insurance. Wasn't it those associations of volunteers that redeemed, for Alexis de Tocqueville, the American experiment, by showing that democracy is not a form of disorder but another kind of order, and one that could reconcile the freedom of the individual with obedience to an overarching law?

The emasculated society of Europe serves, then, as a warning to conservatives, and reinforces their belief that America must reverse the trend of modern politics, which has involved the increasing assumption by the state of powers and responsibilities that belong to civil society. Such has been the call of the Tea Party movement, and it is this same call that animated the

Republican caucus in Congress as it prolonged the fight against Obamacare, to the point where, by jeopardising the fiscal probity of the nation, it antagonised the American people. It is therefore pertinent to consider not only the bad side of government – which Americans can easily recognise – but also the good. For American conservatives are in danger of appearing as though they had no positive idea of government at all, and were in the business simply of opposing all new federal programs, however necessary they may be to the future and security of the nation. Most of all, they seem to be losing sight of the truth that government is not only natural to the human condition, but an expression of those extended loyalties over time, which bind generation to generation in a relation of mutual commitment.

The truth is that government, of one kind or another, is manifest in all our attempts to live in peace with our fellows. We have rights that shield us from those who are appointed to rule us – many of them ancient common-law rights, like that defined by *habeas corpus*. But those rights are real personal possessions only because government is there to enforce them – and if necessary to enforce them against itself. Government is not what so many conservatives believe it to be, and what people on the left always believe it to be when it is in other hands than their own – namely a system of power and domination. Government is a search for order, and for power only in so far as power is required by order. It is present in the family, in the village, in the free associations of neighbours, and in the 'little platoons' extolled by Edmund Burke in his *Reflections on the French Revolution* and by Alexis de Tocqueville, in *Democracy in America*. It is there in the first movement of affection and good will, from which the bonds of society grow. For it is simply the other side of freedom, and the thing that makes freedom possible.

Rousseau told us that we are 'born free', arguing that we have only to remove the chains imposed by the social order, in order to enjoy our full natural potential. Although American conservatives have been sceptical of that idea, and indeed stood against its destructive influence during the time of the 60s radicals, they nevertheless also have a sneaking tendency to adhere to it. They are heirs to the pioneer culture. They idolise the solitary entrepreneur, who takes the burden of his projects on his own shoulders and makes space for the rest of us as we timidly advance in his wake. This figure, blown up to mythic proportions in the novels of Ayn Rand, has, in less fraught varieties, a rightful place in the American story. But the story misleads people into imagining that the free individual exists in the state of nature, and that we become free by removing the shackles of government. That is the opposite of the truth.

We are not, in the state of nature, free; still less are we individuals, endowed with rights and duties, and able to take charge of our lives. We are free by nature because we *become* free, in the course of our development. And this development depends at every point upon the networks and relations that bind us to the larger social world. Only certain kinds of social networks encourage people to see themselves as individuals, shielded by their rights and bound together by their duties. Only in certain conditions are people united in society not by organic necessity but by free consent. To put it simply, the human individual is a social construct. And the emergence of the individual in the course of history is part of what distinguishes our civilisation from so many of the other social ventures of mankind.[2]

Hence we individuals, who have a deep suspicion of government, have a yet deeper need for it. Government is wrapped into the very fibres of our social being. We emerge as individuals because our social life is shaped that way. When, in the first impulse of affection, one person joins in friendship with another, there arises immediately between them a relation of accountability. They promise things to each other. They become bound in a web of mutual obligations. If one harms the other, there is a 'calling to account', and the relation is jeopardised until an apology is offered. They plan things, sharing their reasons, their hopes, their praise and their blame. In everything they do they make themselves accountable. If this relation of accountability fails to emerge then what might have been friendship becomes, instead, a form of exploitation.

Our world displays many political systems in which the basic relation of accountability has either not emerged or been distorted in the interests of family, party, ideology or tribe. If there is a lesson to be learned from the so-called Arab Spring it is surely this: that the governments then overthrown were not accountable to the people on whom they depended for their resources. The Middle Eastern tyrannies have left a void in their wake, since there were no offices, no legal procedures, no customs or traditions that enshrined the crucial relation of accountability on which the true art of government depends – the art of government as we individuals understand it. In the Arab tyrannies there was only power, exercised through family, tribe and confession, and without regard to the individual citizen or to the nation as a whole. In such circumstances getting rid of one tyrant merely opens the door to the next one, while plunging the whole society meanwhile into chaos, as the bullies and the fanatics seize their chance.

In everyday life too there are people who relate to others without making themselves accountable. Such people are locked into the game of domination. If they are building a relationship, it is not a *free* relationship. A free relationship is one that grants rights and duties to either party, and which raises their conduct to the higher level in which mere power gives way to a true mutuality of interests. That is what is implied by the second formulation of Kant's Categorical Imperative, which commands us to treat rational beings as ends and not as means only – in other words to base all our relations on the web of rights and duties. Such free relations are not just forms of affection: they are forms of obedience, in which the will of another person exerts a right to be heard. This, as I read him, is Kant's message: sovereign individuals are also obedient subjects, who face each other 'I' to 'I'.

There are other ways of expressing those truths about our condition. But we see them illustrated throughout human life: in the family, the team, the community, the school and the workplace. People become free individuals by learning to take responsibility for their actions. And they do this through relating to others, subject to subject. The free individuals to whom the Founders appealed were free only because they had grown through the bonds of society, to the point of taking full responsibility for their actions and granting to each other the rights and privileges that established a kind of moral equality between them.

In other words, in our tradition, government and freedom have a single source, which is the human disposition to hold each other to account for what we do. No free society can come into being without the exercise of this disposition, and the freedom that Americans rightly cherish in their heritage is simply the other side of the American habit of recognising the accountability towards others. Americans, faced with a local emergency, combine with their neighbours to address it, while Europeans sit around helplessly until the servants of the state arrive. That is the kind of thing we have in mind, when we describe America as the 'land of the free'. We don't mean a land without government; we mean a land with *this* kind of government – the kind that springs up spontaneously between responsible individuals.

Such a government is not imposed from outside: it grows from within the community as an expression of the affections and interests that unite it. It does not necessarily put every matter to the vote; but it respects the individual participant and acknowledges that, in the last analysis, the authority of the leader derives from the people's consent to be led by him. Thus it was that the pioneering communities of America very quickly made laws for themselves, formed clubs, schools, rescue squads and committees in order to deal with the needs that they could not address alone, but for which they depended on the cooperation of their neighbours. The associative habit that so impressed Tocqueville was not merely an expression of freedom: it was an instinctive move towards government, in which a shared order would contain and amplify the responsibilities of the citizens.

When conservatives grumble against government it is against government that seems to them to be *imposed from outside*, like the government of an occupying power. That was the kind of government that grew in Europe under communism, and which is growing again under the European Union. And it is easy to think that a similarly hostile form of government is growing in America, as a result of the liberal policy of regimenting the American people according to moral beliefs that are to a certain measure alien to them. But this would be a mistake, and – because it is a mistake that so many conservatives make – it is time to warn against it.

Government emerges in small communities as the solution to a problem of coordination. Rules occur, not necessarily as commands delivered by some central authority, but as conventions spontaneously adhered to by everyone – like the conventions of good manners. Nobody objects to the local judge or law-maker who is accountable to the people because he is one of them, or to the local planning committee that invites everyone to have an equal say in its decisions. Hayek and others have studied these forms of 'spontaneous order', of which the common law – the great gift that we English-speakers share – is perhaps the most vivid instance. And their arguments suggest that, as societies get bigger and incorporate more and more territory, more and more distinct forms of life and occupations, so do the problems of coordination increase. There comes a point at which coordination cannot be achieved from below, by the natural willingness of citizens to accommodate the desires and plans of their neighbours. At this point coordination begins to require government from above, by which rules and regulations are laid down for the community as a whole, and enforced by what Weber called a 'monopoly of violence' – in other words a law-enforcing system that tolerates no rival.

That describes our condition. Of course, to say as much is not to undermine the complaint against modern government, which has become too intrusive, too determined to impose habits, opinions and values that are unwelcome to many citizens, and too eager to place obstacles in the way of free enterprise and free association. But those effects are not the result of government. They are the result of the liberal mind-set, which is the mind-set of a substantial and powerful elite within the nation. The business of conservatives is to criticise the ones who are misusing government, and who seek to extend its remit beyond the limits that the rest of us spontaneously recognise. Conservatism should be a *defence* of government, against its abuse by liberals.

This cause has been damaged by the failure of many conservatives to understand the true meaning of the welfare state. During the 20th century it became clear that many matters not previously considered by the political process had arrived on the public agenda. Politicians began to recognise that, if government is to enjoy the consent of those who gain no comparative advantage from their social membership, it must offer some kind of *quid pro quo*. This became apparent in the two world wars, when people from all classes of society were required to fight and if necessary to die. Why should they do this, if membership of the society for which they risked their lives had brought them no evident advantages? The fundamental principle was therefore widely accepted, that the state has a responsibility for the welfare of its more needy citizens. This principle is merely the full-scale version of the belief adhered to by all small societies, that people should be cared for by the community when they are unable to care for themselves.

The emergence of the welfare state was therefore a more or less inevitable result of popular democracy, under the impact of total war. If the welfare state has become controversial in recent times it is not because it is a departure from some natural idea of government. It is rather because it has expanded in a way that undermines its own legitimacy. As we know from both the American and the European examples, welfare policies may lead to the creation of a socially dysfunctional underclass. Sustained without work or responsibilities from generation to generation, people lose the habit of accounting to others, turn their backs on freedom and become locked in social pathologies that undermine the cohesion of society.

That result is the opposite of the one intended, and came about in part because of the left-liberal belief that only the wealthy are accountable, since only they are truly free. The poor, the indigent and the vulnerable are, on that view, inherently blameless, and nothing bad that arises from their conduct can really be laid at their door. They are not responsible for their lives, since they have not been 'empowered' to be responsible. Responsibility for their condition lies with the state. The only question is what more the state should do for them, in order to remedy the defects of which state benevolence is in part the cause.

But that way of seeing things expresses a false conception of government. The responsibilities exercised by government are rooted in the accountability of citizens. When government creates an unaccountable class it exceeds its remit, by undermining the relation on which its own legitimacy depends.

The left-liberal mind-set has therefore led to a conception of government that conservatives view with deep suspicion. In the left-liberal world view – and you see this magisterially embodied in the philosophy of John Rawls – the state exists in order to allocate the social product. The rich are not really rich, because they don't own that stuff. All goods, in left-liberal eyes, are unowned until distributed. And the state distributes the goods according to a principle of 'fairness' that takes no account of the moral legacy of our free agreements or of the moral effects of a state-subsidised under-class.

On the left-liberal view, therefore, government is the art of seizing and then redistributing the good things to which all citizens have a claim. It is not the expression of a pre-existing social order shaped by our free agreements and our natural disposition to hold our neighbour to account. It is the creator and manager of a social order framed according to its ruling doctrine of fairness and imposed on the people by a series of top-down decrees. Wherever this conception prevails government increases its power, while losing its inner authority. It becomes the 'market state' of Philip Bobbitt, which offers a deal to its citizens in return for their taxes, and demands no loyalty or obedience beyond a respect for the agreed terms of the deal.[3]

But such a state no longer embodies the ethos of a nation, and no longer commands any loyalty beyond the loyalty sought by the average chain store. As in the social democracies of Europe, public displays of patriotism, of shared allegiance and pride in the country and its history dwindle to a few desultory spasms, and the political class as a whole begins to be looked upon with sarcasm and contempt. Government ceases to be *ours* and becomes *theirs* – the property of the anonymous bureaucracy on which we all nevertheless depend for our creature comforts.

This change in the phenomenology of government is striking. But it has not yet been completed in America. Ordinary Americans are still able to see their government as an expression of their national unity. They take pride in their flag, in their military, in their national ceremonies and icons. They look for ways to 'join in' the American venture, by giving time, money and energy to local clubs of their own. They want to claim ownership of their country, and to share it with their neighbours. They take time off from their conflicts to reaffirm a shared social and political heritage, and still regard the high offices of state with respect. In crucial matters, they believe, the President does not represent a political party or an ideology but the nation – and that means all of us, united in the spontaneous order that brought us together in this land.

In other words, ordinary Americans have a conception of government that is not only natural, but at variance with the left-liberal idea of the state as a redistributive machine. In attacking that idea, conservatives should make clear that they are reaffirming a real and natural alternative. They are defending government as an expression in symbolic and authoritative forms of our deep accountability to each other.

This does not mean that conservatives are wedded to some libertarian conception of the minimal state. The growth of modern societies has created social needs that the old patterns of free association are no longer able to satisfy. But the correct response is not to forbid the state from intruding into the areas of welfare, healthcare, education and the rest, but to limit its contribution to the point where citizens' initiatives can once again take the lead. Conservatives want a society guided by public spirit. But public spirit grows only among people who are free to act on it, and to take pleasure in the result. Public spirit is a form of private enterprise, and it is killed when the state takes over. That is why private charity has disappeared almost completely from continental Europe, and is thriving today only in the Anglosphere, where common-law justice reminds citizens that they are accountable to others for the freedom that they enjoy.

Conservatives therefore have an obligation to map out the true domain of government, and the limits beyond which action by the government is a trespass on the freedom of the citizen. But it seems to me that they have failed to offer the electorate a believable blueprint for this, precisely because they have failed to see that what they are advocating is not freedom *from* government, but another and better kind of government – a government that embodies all that we surrender to our neighbours, when we join with them as a nation.

4

– The Need for Nations –

T he project of European integration, advanced by politicians and elites of defeated nations, was founded on the belief that nationhood and national self-determination were the prime causes of the wars that had ruined Europe. There were disputes as to who started it: Louis XIV? The French Revolutionaries? Napoleon? Metternich? Talleyrand? Fichte? The Revolutionaries of 1848? The Reactionaries and Monarchists? Bismarck? Garibaldi? Wagner? But, however far back you went, in the eyes of the post-war political survivors, you came across the demon of nationalism, locked in conflict with the pure spirit of Enlightenment. As a result of this founding myth European integration was conceived in one-dimensional terms, as a process of ever-increasing *unity,* under a centralised structure of command. Each increase in central power was to be matched by a diminution of national power.

In other words, the political process in Europe was endowed with a *direction*. It is not a direction that the people of Europe have chosen, and every time they are given the chance to vote they reject it – hence everything is done to ensure that they never have the chance to vote. The process moves towards centralisation, top-down control, dictatorship by unelected bureaucrats and judges, cancellation of laws passed by elected parliaments, constitutional treaties framed without any input whatsoever from the people. In the current debt crisis the European elite – composed largely of the governing circles in France and Germany – assumed the right to depose the elected governments of Greece and Italy and to impose their own henchmen, chosen from the ranks of obedient apparatchiks. In this way, the process is moving always towards imperial government, making very clear that the opposite of the nation state is not Enlightenment but Empire. And only one thing stands opposed to this result, and that is the national sentiments of the European peoples.

As an Englishman and a lover of the civilisation of Rome I am not opposed to Empire. But it is important to recognise what it involves and to distinguish the good from the bad forms of it. In my view the good forms serve to protect local loyalties and customs under a canopy of civilisation and law; the bad forms try to extinguish local customs and rival loyalties and to replace them with a lawless and centralised power. The European Union has elements of both arrangements: but it suffers from one overwhelming defect, which is that it has never persuaded the people of Europe to accept it. Europe is, and in my view has ever been, a civilisation of nation states, founded on a specific kind of pre-political allegiance, which is the allegiance that puts territory and custom first and religion and dynasty second in the order of government. Give them a voice, therefore, and the people of Europe will express their loyalties in those terms. In so far as they have *unconditional* loyalties – loyalties that are a matter of identity rather than agreement – they take a national form.

The political class in Europe does not like this, and as a result has demonised the direct expression of national sentiments. Speak up for Jeanne d'Arc and *le pays réel*, for the 'sceptred isle' and St George, for Lemmenkäinen's gloomy forests and the 'true Finns' who roam in them, and you will be called a fascist, a racist and an extremist. There is a liturgy of denunciation here that is repeated all across Europe by a political elite that affects to despise ordinary loyalties while surreptitiously depending on them. The fact is that national sentiment is, for most ordinary Europeans, the only publicly available and publicly shared motive that will justify sacrifice in the common cause – the only source of obligation in the public sphere that is not a matter of what can be bought and sold. In so far as people do not vote to line their own pockets, it is because they also vote to protect a shared identity from the predations of those who do not belong to it, and who are attempting to pillage an inheritance to which they are not entitled. Philip Bobbitt has argued that one major effect of the wars between nation states in Europe has been the replacement of the nation state with the 'market state' – the state conceived as a firm, offering benefits in exchange for duties, which we are free to join or leave as we choose. (See *The Shield of Achilles.*) If this were true, then the nation, as an identity-forming community, would have lost its leading role in defining political choices and loyalties. Indeed, we would have emerged from the world of political loyalty altogether, into a realm of self-interested negotiations, in which sacrifices are no longer accepted, and perhaps no longer required. But if the present crisis has convinced us of nothing else, it has surely brought home to us that the capacity for sacrifice is the precondition of enduring communities, and that when the chips are down politicians both demand sacrifice and expect to receive it.

We have been made well aware by the Islamists that not everyone accepts the nation as the fount of unconditional loyalty. The followers of Sayyid Qutb tell us that national obedience is a form of idolatry, and that it is to Allah alone that obedience is owed. The European nations have never whole-heartedly accepted that kind of theocratic absolutism, and firmly rejected it at the Treaty of Westphalia. The problem for Europe is that the ensuing centuries of territorial jurisdiction have implanted sentiments that do not fit easily into any kind of imperial ambition. In the circumstances of modern democratic government it is only on behalf of the nation that people are prepared to think outside the frame of self-interest. Hence the new imperial project has entered into conflict with the only source of sentiment upon which it could conceivably draw for its legitimacy. The nation states are not equally stable, equally democratic, equally free or equally obedient to the rule of law. But they alone inspire the obedience of the European people, and without them there is no way that the machinery of the Union can act. By replacing national accountability with distant bureaucracy, that machinery has left people disarmed and bewildered in the face of the current crisis.

We see this clearly in the matter of the common currency. The euro, imposed without proof that the people of the 'Eurozone' had any desire for it, was immediately understood, by many politicians in the Mediterranean, as a way of enlarging the national debt. This was very obviously the case in Greece. Bonds issued in euros would benefit from the strength and probity of the northern economies, and would be regarded as safe bets by investors who would not dream of buying bonds issued in drachmas. And the people of Greece agreed, since nobody alerted them to the cost – the *national* cost – that will be paid, once the Eurozone breaks up, as surely it must. Now that the day of reckoning is approaching, people all across the continent sense the need to prepare themselves for hard times. In a crisis people 'take stock', which means that they retreat to the primary source of their social attachment, and prepare to defend it. They do not do this consciously. But they do it nevertheless, and the futile attempt by the politicians to denounce the 'extremism' of the people whose inheritance they have squandered merely exacerbates the reaction. But the situation is not a happy one, since there is no trans-national idea of Europe to which the politician can appeal by way of identifying an object of loyalty outside the borders of the nation state. The half-century of peace and prosperity has fed upon the European cultural inheritance without renewing it. For it is all but impossible for a European politician to evoke the civilisation of Europe when its source – the Christian Religion – has been expunged from official documents and openly repudiated by the European courts. One ground of the current attacks on the 'nationalist' government of Hungary by the European Commission is that the Hungarians have drawn up a constitution which, in its preamble, describes the Hungarians as a 'Christian nation': two words that have been purged from the official vocabulary of Europe.

Indeed, the European process, because it is committed to denying the validity of national cultures, also denies the validity of the European cultural inheritance upon which they draw. The constitutional treaties and trans-national courts have made a point of granting no favours to the Christian faith or to the morality that has sprung from it. A 'cult of the minority' has been imposed from above, as a kind of rebuke to the people of Europe for being Europeans in spirit. This official multiculturalism has done nothing to reconcile immigrant communities to their new surroundings;

instead it has destroyed much that was confident and joyful in the national cultures of Europe and rejected the Christian pieties in favour of a kind of morose materialism.

The result of official multiculturalism is in fact cultural blindness – an inability to perceive the real cultural distinctions that obtain across the European continent and which are rooted in the custom and history of the nation states. If the architects of the euro had taken national cultures properly into account they would have known that the effect of imposing a single currency on Greece and Germany would be to encourage Greece to transfer its debts to Germany, on the understanding that the further away the creditor the less the obligation to repay. They would have recognised that laws, obligations, and sovereignty don't have quite the same meaning in the Mediterranean as they do on the Baltic, and that in a society used to kleptocratic government the fairest way out of an economic crisis is by devaluation – in other words, by stealing equally from everybody.

Why didn't the architects of the euro know those things? The answer is to be found deep within the European project. Cultural facts were simply *impalpable* to the Eurocrats. Allowing themselves to perceive culture would be tantamount to recognising that their project was an impossible one. This would have mattered less if they had another project with which to replace it. But – like all radical projects – that of the

European Union was conceived without a Plan B. Hence it is destined to collapse and, in the course of its collapse, to drag our continent down. An enormous pool of pretence has accumulated at the centre of the project, while the political class skirmishes at the edges, in an attempt to fend off the constant assaults of reality.

Thus we have to pretend that the long observed distinctions between the Protestant north of our continent and the Catholic and Orthodox south is of no economic significance. Being a cultural fact it is unperceivable, notwithstanding Weber's (admittedly exaggerated) attempt to make it central to economic history. The difference between the culture of common law and that of the *code Napoléon* has likewise been ignored, at the cost of alienating the British and the northern Europeans, for whom law has ever been a social rather than a political product. The distinction between the Roman and the Ottoman legal legacies has been set aside, as has that between countries where law is certain and judges incorruptible and places where law is only the last resort in a system of bribes. Times and speeds of work, and the balance between work and leisure, which go to the heart of every community since they define its relation to time, are ignored, or else regimented by a futile edict from the centre. And everything is to be brought into line by those frightening courts – the European Court of Justice and the European Court of Human Rights – whose unelected judges never pay the cost of their decisions, and whose agenda of 'ever-closer union' and 'non-discrimination' is calculated to wipe away the traces of local loyalties, family-based morality, and rooted ways of life. Not surprisingly, when you build an empire on such massive pretences, it very soon becomes unstable.

We can rescue Europe, it seems to me, only if we can recover the project that Charles de Gaulle wished to place at its heart, and which was effectively scotched by Jean Monnet – the project of a Europe of Nations. It will not be easy to unravel the web of regulations and edicts contained in the 170,000 pages of the *acquis communautaire*; nor will it be easy to redefine the roles and the structures of the European courts and the competences of the European Institutions. But the most difficult thing will be to obtain agreement on what national sovereignty really means. In particular, what will sovereignty mean in the aftermath of the European Union? Conservative politicians in Britain often speak of recapturing powers from Brussels, as though these powers will not have been altered by captivity, and as though they can be easily domesticated when they are brought back home. This is like Menelaus thinking that home life in Mycenae would be just the same when he had returned victorious from Troy, the recaptured Helen obediently trotting behind, as it was in the good old days before she left.

The situation of Europe today reminds us that by conceiving pre-political loyalties in national rather than religious terms, European civilisation has made room for the Enlightenment. The national idea is not the enemy of Enlightenment but its necessary precondition. National loyalty marginalises loyalties of family, tribe and faith, and places before the citizen's eyes, as the focus of his patriotic feeling, not a person or a group but a country. This country is defined by a territory, and by the history, culture and law that have made that territory *ours*. It is the emergence of territory from behind religion, tribe and dynasty that characterises the nationalist art and literature of the nineteenth century, and the national anthems of the self-identifying nations were conceived as invocations of home, in the manner of Sibelius's *Finlandia* or our own unofficial national anthem, 'Land of Hope and Glory'.

In short, Enlightenment means borders. Take away borders, and people begin to identify themselves not by territory and law, but by tribe, race or religion. Nationality is composed of land, together with the narrative of its possession. It is this form of territorial loyalty that has enabled people in Western democracies to exist side by side, respecting each other's rights as citizens, despite radical differences in faith, and without any bonds of family, kinship or long-term local custom to sustain the solidarity between them. For on the foundation of territorial attachment it has been possible to build a kind of civic patriotism, which acknowledges institutions and laws as shared possessions, and which can extend a welcome to those who have entered the social contract from outside. You cannot immigrate into a tribe, a family or a faith; but you can immigrate into a country, provided you are prepared to obey the rules that make that country into a home.

National loyalty is not known everywhere in the world. Consider Somalia. People sometimes refer to Somalia as a 'failed state', since it has no central government capable of making decisions on behalf of the people as a whole, or of imposing any kind of legal order. But the real trouble with Somalia is that it is a failed nation. It has never developed the kind of secular, territorial and law-minded sovereignty that makes it possible for a country to shape itself as a nation state rather than an assemblage of competing tribes and families.

This observation is, of course, pertinent to the Middle East as a whole today, where we find the remnants of a great Islamic Empire divided into nation states. With a few exceptions this division is the result of boundaries drawn on the map by Western powers, and notably by Britain and France as a result of the Sykes-Picot accords of 1917. But the vexed question of Islam and modernity would take us too far from our topic; suffice it to say that tribe and creed have always been more important than sovereignty in Islamic ways of thinking, and the non-emergence of nations in the Middle East is partly explained by this, as is their embryonic emergence in those countries, like Lebanon and Egypt, with substantial Christian minorities, maintaining long-standing trade links with Europe.

I have no doubt that it is the long centuries of Christian dominance in Europe which laid the foundations of national loyalty, as a loyalty above those of faith and family, and on which a secular jurisdiction and an order of citizenship can be founded. It may sound paradoxical, to identify a religion as the major force behind the development of secular government. But we should remember the peculiar circumstances in which Christianity entered the world. The Jews were a closed community, bound in a tight web of religious legalisms, but governed from Rome by a law which made no reference to any God and which offered an ideal of citizenship to which every free subject of the Empire might aspire.

Christ found himself in conflict with the legalism of his fellow Jews, and in broad sympathy with the idea of secular government – hence his famous words in the parable of the Tribute Money: render unto Caesar what is Caesar's and to God what is God's. The Christian faith was shaped by St Paul for the use of communities within the Empire, who wanted only space to pursue their worship, and had no intention of challenging the secular powers. Hence 'the powers that be are ordained of God' (Romans 13). And this idea of dual loyalty continued after Constantine, being endorsed by Pope Gelasius the First in the sixth century, in his doctrine of the two swords given to mankind for their government, that which guards the body politic, and that which guards the individual soul. It is this deep endorsement of secular law by the early Church that was responsible for the subsequent developments in Europe – through the Reformation and the Enlightenment – to the purely territorial law that prevails in the West today.

It is very clear from the history of our continent, that new forms of solidarity have here come into being which owe much to the Christian inheritance, but which are premised on the assumption that legitimacy is a man-made and not a God-bestowed achievement. Nations emerged as forms of pre-political order that contain within themselves the principles that would legitimise sovereign government. Political theorists of the Enlightenment such as Locke and Rousseau tried to encapsulate this legitimising process in a social contract, by which the members of society form an agreement to be governed in a certain way in exchange for renouncing the state of nature. But it is surely obvious that if people assemble to consider a contract that will unite them, it is because they already belong together, already acknowledge that the welfare of each depends upon the actions of all. A contract, however strong its terms, can never establish more than a *conditional* obligation, whereas political order depends, in the end, on an unconditional component, as do marriage and the family. Without this unconditional component no community can survive a real crisis.

The social contract therefore establishes a form of

government that will protect and perpetuate an allegiance that precedes the contract and makes it possible. This allegiance is shaped by history and territory, and by all the forms of association that spring from these, notably language, customary law and religious observance. Seeing things in this way, religious observance is demoted to one factor among others, and is reshaped as a *subject* of law, rather than a source of it. That, to my mind, is the great achievement of European civilisation: to have placed man-made law at the heart of the community, to have subordinated all associations, including those stemming from religion, to the demands of the secular jurisdiction, and to have established the institutions through which law can adapt to changes in social life instead of blurting out some 'eternal' message revealed in circumstances that have vanished, leaving no other trace.

However, law so conceived is territorial and therefore national. It is a law that defines boundaries, beyond which its writ does not run. Claims to jurisdiction from a place outside those boundaries are fiercely resisted, as we know from the history of England and from the conflict between the crown and the papacy that has been decisive in forming many of the nation states of Europe. When it is proposed that the *Corpus Juris,* the EU's foray into establishing European criminal law, should permit European courts to charge British citizens with criminal offences and extradite them to the place most convenient for their trial, it is hardly surprising that British people receive this suggestion with outrage. Their conception of law is the common law conception, which does not permit people to be held indefinitely without trial, and which depends for its authority on the 'law of the land', as embodied in cases decided in the sovereign territory of the English Crown. This attachment of law to territory is not some arbitrary limitation, as though there were a universal jurisdiction from which local jurisdictions are derived by restriction. It is the very essence of law, as the European experience has defined it. We are heirs to a conception of law as arising from the attempt to settle conflicts, to establish institutions, to adjudicate rights and duties, among people who are bound to each other as neighbours. Law, as we know it, is produced by the place that needed it, and is marked by the history of that place. (The contrast with the *Shari'ah* is obvious, as is the contrast with the 'natural law' of the stoics and the Universal Church.)

Hence the attempt to build a European Empire of laws that depend upon no national allegiance for their authority is not merely bound to fail. It is likely also to undermine the authority of secular law in the minds of the European people. There is already in the social contract theories of the eighteenth century a kind of wishful thinking about human nature, a belief that people can reshape all their obligations without reference to their affections, so as to produce an abstract calculus of rights and duties in the place of their contingent and historical ties. The French revolutionaries began their seizure of power in this way, proposing a declaration of the rights of man and the citizen that would sweep away all the arbitrary arrangements of history and place Reason on the throne that had previously been occupied by a mere human being, who had arrived there by the accident of succession. But within weeks of the Declaration the country was being governed in the name of the Nation, the *Patrie*, and the old contingent association was being summoned in another and (to my mind) far more dangerous form, in order to fill the gap in people's affections that had been made by the destruction of customary loyalty, religious usage, and the unquestioned ways of neighbourhood. This was clearly perceived by Burke, who reminded his readers that human beings are thrown together by accidents that they do not choose, and derive their affections not from their decisions but from their circumstances. It is proximity, not reason, that is the foundation of ordinary charitable feeling. Take that thought seriously, and you quickly come to see that territorial forms of association are the best remedy that we have against the divisive call of ideology. National attachment is precisely what prevents 'extremism' from taking hold of the ordinary conscience.

Nationalism is an ideological attempt to *supplant* customary and neighbourly loyalties with something more like a religious loyalty – a loyalty based on doctrine and commitment. Ordinary national loyalty, by contrast, is the by-product of settlement. It comes about because people have ways of resolving their disputes, ways of getting together, ways of cooperating, ways of celebrating and worshipping that seal the bond between them without ever making that bond explicit as a doctrine. This is surely how ordinary people live, and it is at the root of all that is best in human society, namely that we are attached to what goes on around us, grow together with it, and learn the ways of peaceful association as *our* ways, which are right because they are ours and because they unite us with those who came before us and those for whom we will in turn make way. Seen in that way national feelings are not just natural, they are essentially *legitimising*. They call upon the sources of social affection, and bestow that affection on customs that have proved their worth over time, by enabling a community to settle its disputes and achieve equilibrium in the changing circumstances of life.

National sentiments enable people successfully to defend themselves in wartime. But they are also essential in peacetime too. This we are now seeing in Europe, as the sovereign debt crisis begins to affect the lives of ordinary people. Governments are calling on their citizens to make sacrifices for the common good. They are not asking them to make sacrifices for 'Europe', still less for the European Union. If they were to use this language then they would be forced to recognise that Europe is not the bureaucratic machine which has conferred upon them the small measure of legitimacy that they can claim, but a spiritual inheritance that the machine has tried to extirpate. Hence the only invocations that they can make address national sentiments. They speak of the need to pull together, for the sake of *our* community, and at every point their language invokes the contingencies of human affection that make it possible for people to give up something for the sake of others – a habit of mind that social democracies do not normally encourage. They are not speaking the language of nationalism, but the language of attachment, which is something entirely different. Their response to the crisis of Europe reveals that the nation state is not the problem but the solution – it contains within itself the only motives to which politicians can now appeal, when the effects of the European project are finally being felt across the continent.

5

– Building to Last –

T he city, as we have inherited it from the Ancient Greeks, is both an institution and a way of life, one that has been coterminous with the civilisation of Europe. The confluence of strangers in a single place and under a single law, there to live peacefully side by side, joined by social networks, economic cooperation, and friendly competition through sports and festivals, is one of the most remarkable achievements of our species, one that has been responsible for all the great cultural, political and religious innovations of civilisation. Nothing is more precious in the Western heritage, therefore, than the cities of Europe, recording the triumph of civilised humanity not only in their orderly streets, majestic facades and public monuments, but also in the smallest architectural details and the intricate play of light on cornices and apertures.

American visitors to Paris, Rome, Prague or Lisbon, comparing what they see with what is familiar from their own continent, will recognise how careless their countrymen have been, in their spasmodic attempt to create cities. But the American visitor who leaves the route prescribed by the Ministries of Tourism will quickly see that the miracle of a town like

Paris is to be explained only by the fact that few modern architects have been allowed to get their hands on it. Elsewhere European cities are going the way of cities in America: high-rise offices in the centre, surrounded first by a ring of lawless dereliction, and then by the suburbs, to which those who work in the city flee at the end of the day. Admittedly there is nothing in Europe to compare with the vandalism wreaked on Buffalo, Tampa or New Brunswick (to take three cities that have caused me particular pain). Nevertheless the same moral disaster is beginning to afflict us – the disaster of cities in which no one wishes to live, in which public spaces are vandalised and private spaces boarded up.

Until recently European architects have either connived at the evisceration of our cities or actively promoted it. Relying on the spurious rhetoric of Le Corbusier and Gropius, they have endorsed the totalitarian projects of the political elite, whose goal after the war was not to restore the cities but to clear away the 'slums', so completing the work of bombardment. By 'slums' was meant the harmonious classical streets of affordable houses, seeded with local industries, corner shops, schools and places of worship, which had made it possible for real communities to flourish in the centre of our towns. The 'slums' were to be replaced by high-rise blocks in open parkland, of the kind proposed by Le Corbusier in his plan for the demolition of Paris north of the Seine. Meanwhile all forms of employment and enjoyment were to be located elsewhere. Public buildings were to be expressly modernist, with steel and concrete frames and curtain walls, but with no facades or intelligible apertures, and no perceivable relation to their neighbours. Important monuments from the past were to be preserved, but often set in new and aesthetically annihilating contexts, such as that provided for London's St Paul's.

Although citizens protested, and conservation societies fought all across Europe for the old idea of what a city should look like, the modernists won the battle of ideas, took over the schools of architecture, and set out to ensure that the classical discipline of architecture would never again be learned, since it would never again be taught. The vandalisation of the curriculum was successful: students at European schools of architecture are no longer taught the grammar of the classical Orders; they are no longer taught to understand mouldings, to draw existing monuments, urban streets, the human figure or such vital aesthetic phenomena as the fall of light on a Corinthian capital or the shadow of a campanile on a sloping roof; they are no longer taught facades, cornices, doorways or anything else that could be gleaned from a study of the great classical treatises of Serlio and Palladio. The new curriculum has been designed to produce ideologically driven engineers, whose representational skills would go no further than ground plans and isometric drawings, and who would be able to undertake the gargantuan 'projects' required by the socialist state: shovelling people into housing estates, laying out industrial areas and business parks, driving highways through ancient city centres, and generally reminding the middle classes that Big Brother is over-looking them and that they are no longer in charge.

Now all that is changing. The generation that re-belled against socialist planning, rebelled also against the collectivist urbanism of the modernists. The al-ienating architecture of the post-war period was as-sociated in their thinking, and for very good reasons, with the statist politics of socialism. It symbolised the approach to human life of people who believed that they alone had the answers, and that they alone could dictate their answers to the rest of us. The mood of rebellion against this attitude was especially evident in Britain, where the work of the Luftwaffe had in many cities been brought near to completion by the post-war planners. Architects like Quinlan Terry, Liam O'Connor, Demetri Porphyrios and John Simp-son, who grew up amid the advancing chaos, burst the chains forged by their obligatory modernist education and began designing buildings and quarters in a clas-sical style. Meanwhile, working in comparative obscu-rity as an assistant to the eclectic James Stirling, was a graduate of Stuttgart University's modernist school of architecture, Léon Krier, born in Luxembourg in 1946, who was beginning to publish the laconic mono-graphs and satirical drawings that were later to form the basis of an anti-modernist manifesto.

Krier has pursued a career in architecture, but he is also a philosopher and social thinker, who believes that architectural modernism is not just ugly but based in profound mistakes about the nature of human society. As he put it in a recent interview with Nikos Salingaros:

Humanity lives by trial and error, sometimes committing errors of a monumental scale. Architectural and urbanist modernism belong – like communism – to a class of errors from which there is little or nothing to learn or gain. They are ideologies which literally blind even the most intelligent and sensitive people to unacceptable wastes, risks, and dangers. Modernism's fundamental error, however, is to propose itself as a universal (i.e. unavoidable and necessary) phenomenon, legitimately replacing and excluding traditional solutions.

What is needed, therefore, is a repertoire of real solutions to the problems of urban design. And that is what Krier has set out to produce.

During the seventies, with the help of his equally talented brother Rob, Léon Krier began producing designs aimed at showing how the urban fabric of Europe could be conserved, enhanced and expanded, while answering to the real needs of modern people. A few enlightened city councils – notably those of Luxembourg and Bremen – commissioned plans and projects from the Kriers, though largely of an exploratory kind. But it was only in the eighties, when Krier was invited by the Prince of Wales to plan the new town of Poundbury adjacent to the city of Dorchester, that he was granted the opportunity he needed, to put his ideas into practice. His work immediately began to attract the attention of the critics. Professional architects, appalled at the threat to the modernist monopoly, did their best to destroy Krier's reputation, and to dismiss his work as that of a nostalgic dreamer. But, to their consternation, Poundbury has attracted enthusiastic residents, as well as industries and shops; it has become a place of pilgrimage, as popular with tourists as any medieval city, and a model that is being followed elsewhere. The New Urbanist movement, with members in America, Italy, Spain and Britain, owes much to the thinking of Léon Krier, and Krier's credo, *Architecture: Choice or Fate*, published in 1998, is slowly becoming a standard work, although one profoundly hated by the architectural establishment. Krier has worked in America, submitting designs for the New Urbanist development of Seaside, Florida, where he built a house for himself, and also designing the impressive village hall at Windsor, Florida – a new community conceived according to the principles that he defends.

Krier presents the first principle of architecture as a deduction from Kant's Categorical Imperative (which tells us to act only on that maxim which we can will as a universal law). You must 'build in such a way that you and those dear to you will use your buildings, look at them, work in them, spend their holidays in them, and grow old in them with pleasure . . .' The principle is confirmed, Krier suggests, by the modernists themselves. For they all follow the inverse of the famous principle enunciated by Mandeville in *The Fable of the Bees*. Modernist vandals like Richard Rogers and Norman Foster (who between them are responsible for some of the worst acts of destruction in our European cities) live in elegant old houses in charming locations, where artisan styles, traditional materials and humane scales dictate the architectural ambience. Instead of Mandeville's principle – 'private vices, public benefits' – they follow the law of private benefits, public vice. The private benefit of a charming location is paid for by the public vice of tearing our cities apart. Rogers in particular is famous for creating buildings that have no relation to their surroundings, which cannot easily change their use, which are extremely expensive to maintain, and which destroy the character of the neighbourhood – buildings like the Centre Beaubourg in Paris, for which a great acreage of humane streets had to be cleared and which deliberately turns its back on the historic quarter of the Marais, or the Lloyd's Building in London, which is a piece of polished kitchen-ware surmounted by a pile of junk, dumped in the City as though dropped there from an aeroplane.

Traditional architecture produced forms expres-

sive of human interests – palaces, houses, factories,
churches, temples – and these sit easily under their
names. The forms of modern architecture, Krier argues, are nameless – denoting not familiar objects
and their uses but 'so-called objects', objects which
are known at best by a nickname, and never by a real
name of their own. Thus the Berlin Congress Hall is
known as the 'pregnant oyster', Le Corbusier's Unité
d'Habitation in Marseilles as the 'madhouse', the new
building at Queen's College Oxford as the 'parking
lot', and the UN building in New York as the 'radia-
tor'. The nickname, Krier argues, is the correct name
for a kitsch object – i.e. for an object that is faked, and
which sits in its surroundings like a masked stranger at
a family party. Classical forms result from convention
and consensus over centuries; they earn their names
– house, palace, church, factory – from the natural understanding that they elicit, and nothing about them is
forced. The modernist forms, by contrast, have been
imposed upon us by people in the grip of ideology.
They derive no human significance from the materials that compose them, from the labour that produced
them or from the function that they fulfil, and their
monumental quality is merely faked. The skyscraper
office block and landscraper shopping mall speak only
of their specific functions – and this forbids them from
acquiring symbolic value, or from conveying a vision
of the city as a public space.

Krier identifies the leading error of modernism as

that introduced by Corbusier, Gropius and Mies, which was to separate load-bearing and outward facing parts. Once buildings had become curtains hung on invisible frames all the understood ways of creating and conveying meanings were destroyed. Even if the curtain is shaped like a classical façade, it is a fake façade, and one with only a blank expression. Usually, however, it is a sheet of glass or concrete panels, without intelligible apertures. The building itself is hidden, and its posture, as a member of the city, standing among neighbours and resting its weight upon their common ground, is meaningless because unobservable. All relation to neighbouring structures, to the street and to the sky is lost, in a form that has nothing to convey apart from the starkness of its geometry.

The curtain-wall idiom has other negative effects. Buildings constructed in this way are both expensive to maintain and of uncertain durability; they use materials that no one fully understands, which have a coefficient of expansion so large that all joints loosen within a few years, and which involve massive environmental damage in their production and in their inevitable disposal within a few decades as waste. Modernist buildings are ecological as well as aesthetic catastrophes: sealed environments, dependent on a constant input of energy, and subject to the 'sick-building syndrome' that arises when nobody can open a window or let in a breath of fresh air. Moreover, such buildings use no architectural vocabulary, so that they cannot be 'read' as a classical building is read. This 'unreadability' is felt by the passer-by as a kind of rudeness. Modernist buildings exclude dialogue, and the space they create around themselves is not a public space but an unravelling of the urban fabric.

This failure to provide a readable vocabulary is not a trivial defect of the modernist styles: it is the reason why modernist buildings fail to harmonise with their neighbours. In architecture as in music, harmony is a relation between independently meaningful parts, an achievement of order from elements that create and respond to valency. There are no chords in modernist architecture, only lines – lines which may come to an end, but which achieve no closure. The lack of vocabulary also explains the alienating effect of a modern airport, like Newark or Heathrow. Unlike the classical railway station, which guides the traveller securely and reassuringly to ticket office, to platform and to the public concourse, the typical airport has no architectural symbols that carry those meanings on their face. It is a mass of written signs, all competing for attention, all amplifying the sense of urgency yet nowhere offering the point of visual repose. Perhaps the most relaxing and functional public spaces in America are the few classically conceived railway stations – Union Station in Washington, for example, or Grand Central Station, New York – places where architecture has displaced the written sign, and where people, however urgently caught up in travelling, are for the moment content just to be. It is significant that when McKim, Mead and White's great Penn Station, modelled on the baths of Caracalla in Rome, was scheduled for demolition in 1962, even modernists like Louis Kahn joined in the futile protest. The demolition went ahead, since American property law never cedes ground to civic virtue. But it is widely regretted, as much on account of the mean, low-ceilinged space that now alienates the would-be traveller by rail, as of the hideous and oppressive structure on top of it.

Such considerations supplement the criticisms of the 'zoning' idea which, as Jane Jacobs argued in *The Death and Life of Great American Cities*, has been largely responsible for the flight from the centre and the loss of the humane and lived-in street. What makes Krier new, however, and so important for us at the critical point which we have now reached, when everyone apart from professional architects recognises that our cities can be saved only if the centrifugal is replaced by a centripetal force, is that he has a clear and persuasive remedy, one that could easily be adopted by town planners and builders everywhere, and which would be adopted immediately if it were put to the vote.

Krier's solution is to replace the 'downtown plus suburbs' idea with that of the polycentric settlement. If people move out, then let it be to new urban centres, with their own public spaces, public buildings, places of work and leisure: let the new settlements grow, as Poundbury has grown next to Dorchester,

not as suburbs but as towns. For then they will re-
capture the true goal of settlement, which is the human community in a place that is 'ours', rather than
individual plots scattered over a place that is no one's.
They will create a collection of somewheres in place of
the ever-expanding nowhere. This solution has a prec-
edent in London, where the city of London grew next
to the city of Westminster in friendly competition,
and where the residential areas of Chelsea, Kensing-
ton, Bloomsbury and Whitechapel grew as autonomous villages rather than over-spills from the existing
centres. All that is needed to achieve this effect, Krier
argues, is a master plan. By this he does not mean one
of those sinister experiments in social engineering that
appealed to the modernists, but a simple set of side-
constraints, within which people can make the choices
best suited to their needs.

Krier's master plan involves an overall lay-out, a
street plan for each quarter, and rules governing such
things as the shape of plots, the number of floors permitted (five, in Krier's view, is the natural maximum),
and the materials and technical configurations to
which the buildings should conform. The aim is to
control the quality of 'normal, regular and inevitable
building'. At present it is only the exceptional building that attracts the attention of the planners, and the
exceptional building is usually designed, like those of
Daniel Libeskind and Frank Gehry, to stand out rather than to blend in – to focus attention on itself, rather

than on the ordinary solaces of a human community. It is not the exceptional building but the inevitable building that dictates the ambience in which ordinary people work and live. It is here that rules are principally needed, and it is to the shape and aspect of the inevitable building that the old classical pattern-books (such as those by Asher Benjamin and Minard Lafever, used by the original builders of the New England towns) were directed.

The plan should conform to Krier's 'ten-minute rule', meaning that it should be possible for any resident to walk within ten minutes to the places that are the real reason for his living among strangers. This ten-minute rule is not as demanding as Americans might think: Paris, Rome, Florence, Madrid, London and Edinburgh all conform to it, as would the American suburbs if they grew as Krier suggests, as separate centres in a 'polypolis', so that people could work, shop, relax and worship in places close to home. Good urban planning does not mean creating distance between people in the manner of Frank Lloyd Wright's ocean-to-ocean suburbs, but bringing people together in ways that enhance their enjoyment of the *place where they communally are.* That is the goal of the city, and it is, Krier argues, easily achievable. The 'polypolis' will be a network of genuine public spaces, in which the ideal and the fact of communal settlement is recorded in the lie of the street and the genial side-by-sideness of the buildings. Every visible detail should be architectural, Krier argues, since every such detail is part of the public space. Traditional building-styles conformed spontaneously to that principle, since they were controlled by good manners: the builder knew that he was adding to the public space of the town, and that he must conform to its unspoken rules of politeness. As Krier puts it:

All buildings, large or small, public or private, have a public face, a façade; they therefore, without exception, have a positive or negative effect on the quality of the public realm, enriching or impoverishing it in a lasting and radical manner. The architecture of the city and public space is a matter of common concern to the same degree as laws and language – they are the foundation of civility and civilisation. Without their common acceptance there can be no constitution nor maintenance of a normal civilised life. They cannot be imposed and their common rejection is not evidence of misunderstanding but of misconception . . .

That is the vision that Krier has tried to put into effect in Poundbury, where he has worked alongside neo-classical architects like Liam O'Connor and Quinlan Terry to realise his master plan. The town, which is still being built, is conceived as a single and continuous public space, organised around a town hall, each building contributing to the public vistas of which it is a part. It is a small settlement, which will grow in time to 10,000 inhabitants – Krier arguing that beyond that size the need is not for further development around an existing centre, but for another centre. And Poundbury is now a thriving community, in which people live, work and shop, and where residents can walk to everything that they need. It has the feel of a medieval town, though with spaces more suited to our busy age, and a grocery store dealing in the kinds of environmentally friendly product for which the Prince of Wales is a tireless advocate. Poundbury also contains factories and warehouses, as well as offices and civic buildings. The one thing it lacks – though this is indicative of an underlying difficulty in the Krier plan for urban regeneration – is a church. It is not for the architect to provide such a thing, says Krier, but for the residents to demand it. But of course, we should not ignore the fact that the traditional settlements that Krier most admires began from the marking out of a sacred space, and from the building of a temple as a home for the gods. Where God is at home, so too are we; the real meaning of the modernist forms is that there is no God, that meaning has fled from the world, and that Big Brother is now in charge. Krier is inclined to agree; but the problem, he says, is to find ways of building that will enable people to rediscover such truths for themselves. To try to impose a comprehensive vision against the instincts and the plans of ordinary people is simply to repeat the error of the modernists. The true plan for a city is a side-constraint and not a goal.

It is characteristic of our times that Krier's project for urban renewal has been widely dismissed as impractical, despite the evident success of Poundbury. Undeterred by the hostility of the profession Krier continues to expound his vision in lectures, articles and drawings, reminding his audience and his readers that that is what he is doing – *reminding* them. Deep within everyone's psyche, forming the measure of expectations and the image of settlement, is an idea of home, of the somewhere that is not just yours or mine but *ours.* That is the archetype that needs to be reawakened, and which the diseducational policies of the modernists have encouraged us to put out of mind. And, like the laws of logic or the principles of morality, we cannot encounter this idea without being at once persuaded of its obviousness. I have seen Krier lecture to a room full of sceptical left-wingers, who had agreed only reluctantly to listen to this quaint apologist for a vanished age. And with the unassuming, self-questioning manner of a true teacher, he persuaded his audience that the ideas that he laid before them were not his but theirs. They left the room in a condition of stunned self-discovery, understanding their socialist utopias as 'news from nowhere', and committed to somewhere instead. Such is the effect of Krier, I have discovered, on everyone he meets.

Nothing is more striking about him, however, than the feature that distinguishes him among architects – namely, his modesty. He quietly unfolds his schemes for the city of the future, seeking your agreement and appealing for suggestions. His large face and twinkling eyes radiate enthusiasm, and his hands as they unroll his drawings of the imaginary *polis* are the hands of a father gently lifting his new-born baby from the cradle. Although he abhors the modernist vandalism that has torn the hearts out of our cities, he never utters an uncharitable word about those responsible. His whole being is directed towards consensus, towards a democratic pooling of our collective energies, to create the urban environment where we will all be at home. And in his large but placid form you feel the presence of an indefatigable energy, expressing an undaunted love of ordinary humanity.

There are those who say – not of Krier only, but of the whole New Urbanist movement – that it is all very well, but that it comes too late. The centrifugal tendency of the city is now irreversible, and the steel frame and curtain wall are here to stay. Such critics, it seems to me, need to be reminded that sprawl is unsustainable, and will inevitably produce a situation in which centripetal movement is the only alternative to social collapse. And as Quinlan Terry has repeatedly demonstrated, building with steel frame and curtain wall is also unsustainable: structures built in this way quickly become derelict or too costly to maintain, and leave in their wake a quantity of poison that it is now all but impossible to bury. Moreover, they are unadaptable, and can rarely change use as the world around them changes. What the New Urbanists are proposing is not a utopia, but the only viable alternative to continuing urban decline. Of course, as the 20th century – the century of the modernists – teaches us, people have an astonishing ability to march towards catastrophe shouting slogans and waving flags. But why should we endorse that behaviour, when we still retain our critical faculties? Better to ponder Krier's words:

By creating cities, we create ourselves. When we despoil our cities, we despoil ourselves. Our most cherished memories will henceforth generate the poison of regret, of irretrievable loss, even of hatred of what we prized most. We then flee from the world and from ourselves. A beautiful village, a beautiful house, a beautiful city can become a home for all, a universal home. But if we lose this aim we build our own exile here on earth.

Exile is what the collectivist utopias promised; home lies in the opposite direction. Yet it is a direction that our planners and public commissioners still refuse to take. Public projects in our cities are routinely assigned to one of a tiny band of 'starchitects', chosen in order to design structures that will reliably call attention to themselves, and stand out from their surroundings. Most of these starchitects – Daniel Libeskind, Frank Gehry, Richard Rogers, Norman Foster, Zaha Hadid, Peter Eisenman, Rem Koolhaas – have equipped themselves with a store of pretentious gobbledegook, with which to explain their genius to those who are otherwise unable to perceive it.

And when people are spending money that belongs to voters or shareholders, they will be easily influenced by gobbledegook that flatters them into believing that they are spending it on some original and world-changing masterpiece. The victim of this process is the city, and all those who have cherished the city as a home.

There have been architects who are geniuses – Michelangelo, Palladio, Frank Lloyd Wright. But, as Krier has shown, a living city is not the work of geniuses. It is the work of humble craftsmen and also the by-product of its own on-going conversation with itself. A city is a constantly evolving fabric, patched and repaired for our changing uses, in which order emerges by an 'invisible hand' from the desire of people to get on with their neighbours. That is what produces a city like Venice or Paris, where even the great monuments – St Mark's, Nôtre Dame, the Place Vendôme, the Scuola San Rocco – soothe the eye and radiate a sense of belonging. In the past geniuses did their best to harmonise with street, sky and public space – like Bernini at the piazza San Pietro – or to create a vocabulary, as Palladio did, that could become the shared *lingua franca* of a city in which all could be at home.

In contrast, the new architecture, typified by Gehry's costly Guggenheim Museum in Bilbao, by Norman Foster's lopsided City Hall in London, by Richard Rogers's kitchen-utensil Lloyds Building, or by the shiny gadgets of Zaha Hadid, is designed to challenge the surrounding order, and to stand out as the work of some inspired artist, who does not build for people but sculpts space for his own expressive ends. This approach to architecture is encouraged by the professional bodies and the schools, such as the remorselessly trendy Architectural Association and the RIBA. We should not be surprised, therefore, if the 'works of genius' which our city planners are constantly permitting or commissioning have the appearance of things *other* than architecture: of vegetables, vehicles, hairdryers, washing machines or backyard junk. That which makes a building into architecture, which is the ability to embellish a location, and to enhance it as a home, is the aspect of building that architects no longer learn.

It is often argued that the modern constraints make it all but impossible for architects to behave as their predecessors did, veneering buildings with some eclectic reminiscence of the classical or Gothic styles, placing dressed stone over iron frames, or crowning the street façade with a Vignolesque cornice in tin. What were once cheap solutions to a shared public demand for ornament and order, have become forbidding costs. Space is limited, skilled labour rare and gargantuan engineering well understood and relatively inexpensive: and that is why we look to the starchitects, since they authorise what would otherwise look like vandalism on a massive scale.

The typical starchitect building is without a façade

or an orientation that it shares with its neighbours. It often seems to be modelled like a domestic utensil, as though to be held in some giant hand. It does not fit into a street or stand happily next to other buildings. In fact it is designed as waste – throw-away architecture involving vast quantities of energy-intensive materials, which will be demolished within 20 years. Townscapes built from such architecture resemble land-fill sites – scattered heaps of plastic junk from which the eye turns away in dejection. Gadget architecture is dropped in the townscape like litter, and neither faces the passer-by nor includes him. It may offer shelter, but it cannot make a home. And by becoming habituated to it we lose one fundamental component in our respect for the earth. For that, in the end, is what the true city is: a consecration of the earth beneath it.

6

– Effing the Ineffable –

Aquinas, who devoted some two million words to spelling out, in the *Summa Theologica*, the nature of the world, God's purpose in creating it and our fate in traversing it, ended his short life (short by our standards, at least) in a state of ecstasy, declaring that all that he had written was of no significance beside the beatific vision that he had been granted, and in the face of which words fail. His was perhaps the most striking example of a philosopher who comes to believe that the real meaning of the world is ineffable. Having got to this point, Aquinas obeyed the injunction of Wittgenstein, whose *Tractatus Logico-Philosophicus* concludes with the proposition: 'that whereof we cannot speak we must consign to silence'. But Aquinas was exceptional. The history of philosophy abounds in thinkers who, having concluded that the truth is ineffable, have gone on to write page upon page about it. One of the worst offenders is Kierkegaard, who argues in a hundred ways that the ultimate is inexpressible, that truth is 'subjectivity', that the meaning of life can be given by no formula, no proposition, no abstraction, but only by the concrete experience of surrender whose content can never be given in words.

The same idea occurs in Schopenhauer, for whom the truth of the world is Will, which cannot be represented in concepts. Schopenhauer devoted roughly 500,000 words to this thing that no words can capture. And he set a fashion that continues to this day. For example, there is a mercifully short book by Vladimir Jankélévitch, *Music and the Ineffable*, in which the argument is stated on the first page – namely, that since music works through melodies, rhythms and harmonies and not through concepts, it contains no messages that can be translated into words. There follows 50,000 words devoted to the messages of music – often suggestive, poetic and atmospheric words, but words nevertheless, devoted to a subject that no words can capture.

The temptation to take refuge in the ineffable is not confined to philosophers. Every enquiry into first principles, original causes and fundamental laws, will at some stage come up against an unanswerable question: what makes those first principles true or those fundamental laws valid? What explains those original causes or initial conditions? And the answer is that there is no answer – or no answer that can be expressed in terms of the science for which those laws, principles and causes are bedrock. And yet we want an answer. So how should we proceed?

There is nothing wrong with referring at this point to the ineffable. The mistake is to describe it. Jankélévitch is right about music. He is right that

something can be meaningful, even though its meaning eludes all attempts to put it into words. Fauré's F
sharp *Ballade* is an example: so is the smile on the face
of the Mona Lisa; so is the evening sunlight on the
hill behind my house. Wordsworth would describe
such experiences as 'intimations', which is fair enough,
provided you don't add (as he did) further and better
particulars. Anybody who goes through life with open
mind and open heart will encounter these moments of
revelation, moments that are saturated with meaning,
but whose meaning cannot be put into words. These
moments are precious to us. When they occur it is as
though, on the winding ill-lit stairway of our life, we
suddenly come across a window, through which we
catch sight of another and brighter world – a world to
which we belong but which we cannot enter.

I too am tempted to eff the ineffable. Like my
philosophical predecessors, I want to describe that
world beyond the window, even though I know that it
cannot be described but only revealed. I am not alone
in thinking that world to be real and important. But
there are many who dismiss it as an unscientific fiction. And people of this scientistic cast of mind are
disagreeable to me. Their nerdish conviction that facts
alone can signify, and that the 'transcendental' and
the eternal are nothing but words, mark them out as
incomplete. There is an aspect of the human condition that is denied to them. Moreover, this aspect is of
the first importance. Our loves and hopes in some way

hinge on it. We love each other as angels love, reaching for the unknowable 'I'; we hope as angels hope: with our thoughts fixed on the moment when the things of this world fall away and we are enfolded in 'the peace which passes understanding'. Putting the point that way I have already said too much. For my words make it look as though the world beyond the window is actually here, like a picture on the stairs. But it is not here; it is there, beyond the window that can never be opened.

But a question troubles me as I am sure it troubles you. What do our moments of revelation have to do with the ultimate questions? When science comes to a halt, at those principles and conditions from which explanation begins, does the view from that window supply what science lacks? Do our moments of revelation point to the cause of the world? When I don't think about it, the answer seems clear. Yes, there is more to the world than the system of causes, for the world has a meaning and that meaning is revealed. But no, there is no path, not even this one, to the cause of the world: for that whereof we cannot speak, we must consign to silence – as Aquinas did.

7

– Hiding behind the Screen –

M any observers would say that social network-ing sites like Facebook provide a psychological benefit, helping those who are too shy to present themselves directly to the world nevertheless to have a public place and an identity within it. These sites also enable people to keep in touch with a wide circle of friends and colleagues, so multiplying the range of their affections, and filling the world with good will and positive feelings. In so far as any research has been conducted into the opinions of those who use friend-ship and networking sites, the verdict has been largely positive, with the University of Southern California's Annenberg Center for the Digital Future (admittedly, not an unbiased source) declaring, in its sixth annual report, that the Internet is now showing its potential, as a personal and social tool.

Yet something new is entering the world of human relations with these innocent-seeming sites. There is the ease with which people can make contact with each other through the screen. No more need to get up from your desk and make the journey to your friend's house. No more need for the weekly meetings, or the circle of friends in the downtown bar or restaurant.

All those effort-filled ways of making contact can be dispensed with: a touch of the keyboard, and you are there, where you wanted to be, on the site that defines your friend. Can this be real friendship, when it is pursued and developed in such facile and costless ways? The Annenberg Center's report tells us happily that a full twenty per cent of those who participate in on-line communities also participate in off-line activities related to those communities at least once a year. Think of that, at least once a year! Or think of it in another way. A full eighty per cent of those who participate in on-line communities have no face-to-face dealings at all, not even once a year, with those whom they count among their friends.

You can take the evidence either way. Of course real friendship shows itself in action and affection. The real friend is the one who comes to the rescue in your hour of need; who is there with comfort in adversity and who shares with you his own success. This is hard to do on the screen – the screen, after all, is a source of information, not action. No hand reaches from it to comfort the sufferer, to offer financial assistance or to ward off an enemy's blows, though one user of the blogging site Profy informs us that someone with whom he had played Internet games for a couple of years sent him $1,500 when he was in a bind. This kind of spontaneous gesture is possible in any kind of relationship, of course. But it is arguable that the more people satisfy their need for companionship through relationships established on the screen, the less will they develop friendships of that other kind, the kind that offers help and comfort in the real trials of human life. Friendships that exist on the screen cannot easily be lifted off it, and when they are so lifted, there is no guarantee that they will take any strain. Indeed, it is precisely their cost-free, screen-friendly character that attracts many people to them – so much so, that Facebook becomes an addiction, and people often have to forbid themselves to go to their Facebook page for days on end, in order to get on with their real lives and their real relationships.

Indeed, as Christine Rosen has cogently argued, an entirely new conception of friendship is emerging through these networking sites. A person's friends are posted on his site, in the form of links to sites of their own. And each of these sites consists in a display of tastes, hobbies, photographs, and further links to friends. And that might be all that friendship consists in. The site exists not to *exercise* friendship but simply to lay claim to it; people strive to 'collect' friends, and their self-esteem rises with the number of friends linked to their site. Each site has one purpose above all others, which is to put its owner on display. As Rosen puts it, the Delphic maxim 'know thyself', which for the Greeks was the heart of meaningful social relations, has been replaced by another: 'show thyself'. And friendship comes about simply by showing yourself in the company of another. Little suggests that friendship is a sphere of activity, still less a sphere of duty. This is a duty-free world, in which we all stand side-by-side on display, like chorus girls.

Of course, friendships formed on-line can also be pursued off-line, in that dangerous world of real activities and real desires. And then the new opportunities for deception and predation reveal themselves. We already know how vulnerable children and young people are to those who prowl around the Internet chat-rooms. Every kind of lie about yourself can easily be made on the screen: the lying biography, lying photograph, lying address, lying statement of intent – none of these can be easily detected until that face-to-face encounter in circumstances chosen by the predator, by which time it is too late. Of course, nothing here is entirely new: dating agencies have always been exploited by those looking for sexual victims, and people have laid traps by letter since the beginning of literacy. Nevertheless, the opportunity exists to create a virtual personality, and to step down into the real world to take possession of assets deceitfully acquired and inadequately protected.

What we are witnessing is a change in the *attention* that mediates and gives rise to friendship. In the once normal conditions of human contact, people became friends by being in each other's presence, understanding all the many subtle signals, verbal and bodily, whereby another testifies to his character, emotions and intentions, and building affection and trust in tandem. Attention was fixed on the other – on his face, words and gestures. And his nature as an embodied person was the focus of the friendly feelings that he inspired. People building friendship in this way are strongly aware that they appear to the other as the other appears to them. The other's face is a mirror in which they see their own. Precisely because attention is fixed on the other there is an opportunity for self-knowledge and self-discovery, for that expanding freedom in the presence of the other which is one of the joys of human life. The object of friendly feelings looks back at you, and freely responds to your free activity, amplifying both your awareness and his own. In short friendship, as traditionally conceived, was ruled by the maxim 'know thyself'.

When attention is fixed on the screen, however, there is a marked shift in emphasis. For a start I have my finger on the button. At any moment I can turn the image off, or flick to some new encounter. The other is free in his own space, but he is not really free in mine, since he is entirely dependent on my decision to keep him there. I retain ultimate control, and in an important sense am not risking myself in the friendship as I risk myself when I meet the other face to face. Of course, the other may so grip my attention with his messages, images and requests, that I stay glued to the screen. Nevertheless, it is a *screen* that I am glued to, and not the face that I see in it. All interaction with the other is at a distance, and can affect me only if I choose to be affected. Over this person I enjoy a power of which he himself is not really aware – since he is not aware of the extent of my desire to retain his presence in the space before me. He too, therefore, will not risk himself; he appears on the screen only on condition of retaining that ultimate control. This is something I know about him that he knows that I know – and vice versa. There grows between us a reduced-risk encounter, in which each is aware that the other is fundamentally *withheld*, sovereign within his impregnable cyber-castle.

But that is not the only way in which cyber-relationships are affected by the medium of their formation. Everything that appears on the screen appears in competition with whatever else might be called up by the mouse. You 'click on' your friend, as you might click on a news item, a music video, or a fragment of film. He is one of the many products on display. Friendship with him, and relationship generally, belongs in the category of amusements and distractions, a commodity that may or may not be chosen, depending on the rival goods. This contributes to a radical demotion of the personal relationship. Your friendships are no longer special to you, and definitive of your moral life: they are amusements – what Marxists would call 'fetishes', things that have no real life of their own but borrow their life from your interest in them.

As I said, there is a strong argument for saying that the Facebook experience, which has attracted millions of people from all around the world, is an antidote to shyness, a way in which people otherwise cripplingly intimidated by the venture outwards into society, are able to overcome their disability and enjoy the web of affectionate relationships on which so much of our happiness depends. But there is an equally strong argument that holds that the Facebook experience hypostatises shyness, retains its principal features, while substituting an ersatz kind of affection for the real affection that shyness fears. For by placing a screen between yourself and the friend, while retaining ultimate control over what appears on that screen, you also hide from the real encounter – forbidding to the other the power and the freedom to challenge you in your deeper nature and to call on you here and now to take responsibility for yourself and for him.

I was taught that shyness is not a virtue but a defect, and that it comes from placing too high a value on yourself – a value that forbids you to risk yourself in the encounter with others. I think there is truth in this diagnosis. But it is a truth that supports an argument against the Facebook experience. By removing the *real* risks from interpersonal encounters the Facebook experience might encourage a kind of narcissism, a self-regarding posture in the midst of what should have been other-regarding friendship. In effect there may be nothing more than the display of self, the others listed on the website counting for nothing in themselves.

In its normal occurrence, however, the Facebook encounter is still an encounter – however attenuated – between real people. We are now beginning to witness the next stage in screen addiction, in which the screen finally takes over – ceasing to be a means of communication between real people who exist elsewhere, and becoming the place where people finally achieve reality, the only place where they relate in any coherent way to others. I am thinking of the new 'avatar' phenomenon, in which people create their own screen substitutes, whose life on the screen is one to which all personal relationships are consigned, so enabling their controllers to live in complete self-complacency behind the screen, exposed to no danger and yet enjoying a kind of substitute affection through the adventures of their cyber-child. Already Second Life, which offers a virtual world and invites you to enter it in the form of an avatar taken from its collection of templates, has 100 million or more users worldwide. It has its own currency, in which purchases can be made in its own stores; it rents spaces to avatars as their homes and businesses. It also provides opportunities for 'social' action, with social positions achieved by merit, or at any rate virtual merit. In this way people can enjoy, through their avatars, cost-free versions of the social emotions, become heroes of 'compassion', without lifting a finger in the real world. Some nations already have embassies in Second Life, which your avatar can visit to obtain advice about immigration, trade and politics.

In one notorious recent incident one avatar attempted to sue another for the theft of a copyright idea; and lurking just round the corner in the avatar world is the ever-growing temptation of pornography, with avatar sites now available in which your cyber-child can realise your wildest fantasies, at no risk to yourself. On You-tube it is possible to see a film in which a couple who have never met describe their adulterous affair conducted in cyber-space, showing no guilt towards the victim, and proudly displaying their narcissistic emotions as though they had achieved some kind of moral breakthrough, by ensuring that it is only their avatars, and not they themselves, that ended up in bed together.

This might be the model that many will follow: no risk adultery. John gives cyber-birth to Johngo, an avatar with all the qualities that John would wish for but lacks: Johngo is strong, handsome, fearless and energetic, though deficient in intellect since of necessity he cannot be brainier than his creator. John stays all day glued to the screen, propelling Johngo through cyber-space in search of the encounters that will test his courage and bring him renown. Mary, meanwhile, has given birth to her own beautiful, graceful and man-killing avatar, Masha, compensating for Mary's own life as an obese and man-fearing chocaholic by releasing her pent-up yearnings in Masha's promiscuous lust. Johngo and Masha meet: how could they fail to be impressed by each other? The brainless stud and the manipulating tart begin a relationship which at any moment can be cut off at source, when either John or Mary gets tired of the performance. If it continues, it is only because John and Mary enjoy the fantasy of a relationship that neither of them possesses; if it stops it is without heartbreak, since there are no hearts to break. Yet both John and Mary know that their avatars have no other future. Johngo and Masha have each met their nemesis; and their routine can go on forever, stuck in the groove of fantasies that control the screen.

I think most people would see this as an unhealthy state of affairs. It is one thing to place a screen between yourself and the world; it is another thing to inhabit that screen as the unique sphere of your relationships. In vesting your emotional life in the adventures of an avatar you are retreating from real relationships completely. Instead of being the means to amplify relationships that exist outside of it, the computer could become the sole arena of social life – but an unreal life involving unreal people. The nerd controlling the avatar has essentially 'put his being outside of himself', and the thought of this awakens all those once fashionable critiques of alienation and the fetishism of commodities, with which Marx and his followers castigated capitalist society. It provides us with an opportunity to revisit those critiques, to see whether there is anything of truth to be discovered in them.

The origin of those old critiques lies in an idea of Hegel's, and it is an idea of enduring importance, which is constantly resurging in new guises, especially in the writings of psychologists concerned to map the contours of ordinary happiness. The idea is this: we human beings fulfil ourselves through our own free actions, and through the consciousness that these bring of our individual worth. But we are not free in a state of nature, nor do we, outside the world of human relations, have the kind of consciousness of self that allows us to value and intend our own fulfilment. Freedom is not reducible to the unhindered choices that even an animal might enjoy; nor is self-consciousness simply a matter of the pleasurable immersion in immediate experiences, like the rat pressing endlessly on the pleasure switch. Freedom involves an active engagement with the world, in which opposition is encountered and overcome, risks are taken and satisfactions weighed: it is, in short an exercise of practical reason, in pursuit of goals whose value must justify the efforts needed to obtain them. Likewise self-consciousness, in its fully realised form, involves not merely an openness to present experience, but a sense of my own existence as an individual, with plans and projects that might be fulfilled or frustrated, and with a clear conception of what *I* am doing, for what purpose and with what hope of happiness.

All those ideas are contained in the term first introduced by the German post-Kantian philosopher, J. G. Fichte, to denote the inner goal of a free personal life: *Selbstbestimmung* or self-certainty. The crucial claim of Hegel is that the life of freedom and self-certainty can only be obtained through others. I become fully myself only in contexts which compel me to recognise that I am another in others' eyes. I do not acquire my freedom and individuality and then, as it were, try them out in the world of human relations. It is only by entering that world, with its risks, conflicts and responsibilities, that I come to know myself as free, to enjoy my own perspective and individuality, and to become a fulfilled person among persons. In the *Phenomenology of Spirit* and the *Philosophy of Right*, Hegel tells many pleasing and provocative parables about the way in which the subject achieves freedom and fulfilment through his *Entäusserung* – his objectification – in the world of others. And the status of these parables – whether they are arguments or allegories, conceptual analyses or psychological generalisations – has always been a matter of dispute. But I don't think any psychologist now would dispute the fundamental claim that underpins them, which is that the freedom and fulfilment of the self come about only through the recognition of the other. Without others my freedom is an empty cipher, and recognition of the other involves taking full responsibility for my own existence as the individual who I am.

In his efforts to 'set Hegel on his feet', the young Marx drew an important contrast, between true freedom, that comes to us through relationship with other subjects, and the hidden enslavement that comes when our ventures outwards are not towards subjects but towards objects. In other words, he suggested, we must distinguish the realisation of the self, in free relations with others, from the alienation of the self in the system of things. That is the core of his critique of private property, and it is a critique that is as much bound up with allegory and storytelling as the original Hegelian arguments. And in later writings the critique is transformed into the theory of 'fetishism', according to which people lose their freedom through making fetishes of commodities. A fetish is something that is animated by a *transferred* life. The consumer in a capitalist society, according to Marx, transfers his life into the commodities that bewitch him, and so loses that life, becoming a slave to commodities precisely through seeing the market in goods, rather than the free interactions of people, as the place where his desires are brokered and fulfilled.

Let me say that I do not endorse those critiques of property and the market, and see them as flamboyant off-shoots of a philosophy which, properly understood, endorses free transactions in a market as much as it endorses free relations between people generally, indeed seeing the one as no more than an application of the other. However, this is not directly relevant to my theme, which is the idea of the *Entäusserung*, the realisation, of the self through responsible relations with others. This, it seems to me, is the core contribution of German romantic philosophy to the understanding of the modern condition, and it is an idea that has direct application to the problems that we see emerging in our new world of internet addiction. It seems to me incontrovertible that, in the sense in which freedom is a value, freedom is also an artefact, which comes into being through the mutual interaction of people. This mutual interaction is what raises us from the animal to the personal condition, enabling us to take responsibility for our lives and actions, to evaluate our goals and character, and both to understand the nature of personal fulfilment and to set about desiring and intending it. This process is crucial, as the Hegelians emphasised, to the growth of the human subject, as a self-knowing agent, capable of entertaining and acting from reasons, with a developed first-person perspective and a sense of his reality as one subject among others. It is a process that depends upon real conflicts and real resolutions, in a shared public space where we are each accountable for what we are and do. Anything that interferes with that process, by undermining the growth of inter-personal relations, by confiscating responsibility, or by preventing or discouraging an individual from making long-term rational choices and adopting a concrete vision of his own fulfilment, is an evil. It may be an unavoidable evil; but it is an evil all the same, and one that we should strive to abolish if we can.

And it is undeniable that there are ways in which we damage or retreat from this process of self-realisation, and that Internet addiction is only one of them. Long before that addiction arose, and preparing the way for it, was the television addiction, which corresponds exactly to the Hegelian and Marxist critique of the fetish – an inanimate thing in which we invest our life, and so lose it. Of course we retain ultimate control over the television: we can turn it off. But people don't, on the whole, and remain fixed to the screen in all those moments when they might otherwise be building relationships, through conversation, activities, conflicts and projects. The television has, for a vast number of our fellow human beings, destroyed family meals, home cooking, hobbies, homework, study, and family games such as charades. It has rendered many people largely inarticulate, and deprived them of the simple ways of making direct conversational contact with their fellows. I am not referring simply to TV's 'dumbing down' of thought and imagination, or its manipulation of people's desires and interests through brazen imagery. Those features are familiar enough, and the constant target of despairing criticism. Nor am I referring only to its addictive quality – though research by the psychologists Mihaly Csikszentmihalyi and Robert Kubey establishes beyond doubt that TV is addictive in the same way as gambling and drugs.

I am referring to the nature of television as a replacement for relationships. By watching people interacting on the TV sitcom the addict is able to dispense with interactions of his own. Those energies and interests that would otherwise be focused on others, in story-telling, arguing, singing together or playing games, in walking, talking, eating and acting, are consumed on the screen, in vicarious lives that involve no engagement of the viewer's own moral equipment. And that equipment therefore atrophies. We see this everywhere in modern life, but nowhere more vividly than in the students who arrive in our colleges. These divide into two kinds – those from TV-sodden homes, and those who have grown up talking. Those of the first kind tend to be reticent, inarticulate, given to aggression when under stress, unable to tell a story or express a view, and seriously hampered when it comes to taking responsibility for a task, an activity or a relationship. Those of the second kind are the ones who step forward with ideas, who go out to their fellows, who radiate the kind of freedom and adventurousness that makes learning a pleasure and risk a challenge. Many of these TV-free young people are home-schooled, or products of the Bible belt, used to singing hymns and saying prayers at home: and of course this means that they are often mocked by their liberal professors who despise the Bible belt, not seeing that it is the Bible belt that keeps up America's trousers. But in my experience these students have a head start over their TV-addicted contemporaries. The latter can, indeed, be freed from their vice, and the purpose of university sport, theatre, music and so on is in part to make the campus a place where TV is marginalised. But in many other public or semi-public spaces TV has now become a near necessity: it flickers in the background, reassuring those who have bestowed their life on it that their life goes on. The correct response to this kind of addiction is not to attack those who manufacture TVs or who stock them with rubbish: it is to concentrate on the kind of education that makes it possible to take a critical approach to TV, so as to demand real insight and real emotion, rather than kitsch, Disney or porn. And the same goes for the iPod.

To work towards this critical approach means getting clear about the virtues of *direct* rather than vicarious relations. Why do we go to the trouble of living, rather than, as Villiers de Lisle Adam said, asking our servants to do it for us? Why do we criticise those who eat burgers on the couch, while life plays out its pointless drama on the screen? Get clear about these questions, and we can begin to educate children in the art of turning off the television.

We are rational beings, endowed with practical as well as theoretical reasoning. And our practical reasoning develops through the confrontation with risk and uncertainty. In an important sense life on the screen is risk free, and – although we can make the decision to turn it off or click on another bauble – we risk nothing immediate in the way of physical danger, emotional embarrassment, or accountability to others when we click to enter some new domain. You can decide to 'kill' your screen identity at any time, and you will suffer nothing as a consequence. Why, then, trouble to enter the world of real encounters, when this easy substitute is available? And when the substitute becomes a habit, the virtues needed for the real encounter do not develop.

Now it should not go unmentioned that the habit of reducing risk is one that is widespread in our society, and indeed encouraged by governments. An unhealthy obsession with health and an unsafe craze for safety have confiscated many of the risks that previous generations have not merely taken for granted but incorporated into the process of moral education. From the padding of children's playgrounds and the mandating of helmets for skateboarders to the criminalisation of wine at the family table, the health and safety fanatics have surrounded us at every point with a web of prohibitions, while encouraging the belief that risks are not the concern of the individual but a matter of public policy. Children are not, on the whole, encouraged to risk themselves in physical ways; and it is not surprising if they are reluctant, in consequence, to risk themselves in emotional ways either.

However, I do not think that this is either the source of risk-avoidance in human relationships, or a real indication of the right and the wrong way to proceed. No doubt children need physical risk and adventure if they are to develop as responsible people, with their full quota of courage, prudence and practical wisdom. But risks of the soul are unlike risks of the body.

You don't learn to manage them by being exposed to them: on the contrary. As we know, children exposed to sexual predation do not learn to deal with it but, on the contrary, acquire the habit of *not* dealing with it: of closing off the sexual side of life altogether, reducing it to a raw, angry bargaining, learning to treat themselves as objects and losing the capacity to risk themselves in love.

Risk-avoidance in human relations means the avoidance of *accountability*, the refusal to stand *judged* in another's eyes, to come *face to face* with another person, to give yourself in whatever measure to him or her, and so to run the risk of rejection. Accountability is not something we should avoid; it is something we need to learn. Without it we can never acquire either the capacity to love or the virtue of justice. Other people will remain for us merely complex devices, to be negotiated in the way that animals are negotiated, for our own advantage and without opening the possibility of mutual judgement. Justice is the ability to see the other as having a claim on you, as being a free subject just as you are, and as demanding your accountability. To acquire this virtue you must learn the habit of face-to-face encounters, in which you solicit the other's consent and cooperation rather than imposing your will. The retreat behind the screen is a way of retaining complete control of the encounter, while never acknowledging the other's point of view. It involves setting your will outside yourself, as a feature of virtual reality, while not risking it as it must be risked, if others are truly to be encountered. To encounter another person in his freedom is to acknowledge his sovereignty and his right: it is to recognise that the developing situation is no longer within your exclusive control, but that you are caught up by it, made real and accountable in the other's eyes by the same considerations that make him real and accountable in yours.

Perhaps we can survive in a world of virtual relations; but it is not a world into which children can easily enter, except as intruders. Avatars may reproduce on the screen: but they will not fill the world with real human children. And the cyber-parents of these avatars, deprived of all that makes people grow as moral beings – of risk, embarrassment, suffering and love – will shrink to mere points of view, on a world in which they do not really occur.

8

– Mourning Our losses –

REFLECTIONS ON STRAUSS'S *METAMORPHOSEN*

In a significant essay entitled 'Mourning and Melancholia', Freud writes of 'the work of mourning', meaning the psychic process whereby a cherished object is finally laid to rest, as it were buried in the unconscious, and the ego liberated from its grip. Until the work of mourning has been accomplished, Freud argues, new life, new loves, new engagement with the world are all difficult if not impossible. This is the explanation, as he sees it, of the state that used to be known as melancholia – a kind of willed helplessness in which the world is seen as alien and unmanageable.

I am not, in general, persuaded by Freudian psychology. But in this matter, it seems to me, Freud was on the right lines. We lose many things in our lives. But some losses are existential losses. They take away some part of what we are. After such a loss we are in a new and unfamiliar world, in which the support on which we had – perhaps unknowingly – depended is no longer available. The loss of a parent, especially during one's early years, is a world-changing experience, and orphans are marked for life by this. The loss of a spouse can be equally traumatic, as is the loss of children, who take with them into the void all the most tender feelings of their parents. Such losses leave us helpless, and even if we find a way of healing the wounds that they make, the scars will remain.

Religions, laws and customs all provide for the ritual mourning of beloved people. But there are no clear precedents for the work of mourning, when what is mourned is a nation, a civilisation or a place. And if it is true that Strauss was mourning, in *Metamorphosen*, the Germany that he had known, and which had been destroyed by the Second World War, then there is an added problem that he must certainly have encountered, which is the great difficulty we all have, in mourning what we condemn. The work of mourning, as Freud conceived it, is a work of redemption, in which the lost figure is blessed in the memory of the one he leaves behind. All funeral rites, and all elegies for the dead are designed to highlight the virtues and to minimise the vices of the departed person. Mourning is a process of reconciliation, a work of forgiveness, in which the dead person is retrospectively granted the right to die. But what if the departed person cannot be forgiven? What if his vices are an immovable obstacle to all attempts to accept him? Then mourning becomes impossible.

Germans after the war felt this about their country. The Germany that we know from art, music and literature – the Germany of the Gothic cathedrals and the gingerbread cities, of Dürer and Grünewald, of Luther's Bible, of Goethe, Schiller, Kant and Hegel, the Germany of the romantic poets and of the greatest continuous musical tradition that the world will ever know – that Germany had been poisoned in people's thoughts by Hitler. It would have been easier to deal with the memory of the Hitler years, if they had been imposed on Germany by some alien power which had sought to obliterate this great nation, as the Mongols obliterated the civilisation centred on Baghdad, or as the Chinese are at this moment obliterating Tibet. But it was not like that. The Nazis proclaimed themselves heirs to German civilisation. Hitler was not just a madman: he was an aesthete and an intellectual, like Stalin and Mao; he emphasised in all his speeches the history and achievements of the German people; he invoked the art, music and philosophy of Germany as justifications for his cause and objects of his pride. And the Germans followed him on his path of conquest, sharing his triumphs and forced very soon to share his disastrous defeat. Although their music was not destroyed by the war, their cities – the greatest cities in Europe – were reduced to rubble, their civilian population exposed to the horrors of blanket bombing and the rapine of the Soviet Army, and the noses of the survivors rubbed in the unspeakable reality of the holocaust. Their country was destroyed, but it was impossible to mourn it.

Two psychoanalysts, the husband and wife pair Margarete Nielsen and Alexander Mitscherlich, reflected on this situation in a book published in

1967 – *Die Unfähigkeit zu trauern* – the Impossibility of Mourning. The Germans could not grieve for their dead and at the same time accept the guilt that their dead had incurred. Even the heroic self-sacrifice of the German armies on the Russian front could not be given as a proof of virtue. All were guilty – guilty not only for the insane destruction of their country, but also for the crimes against humanity and civilisation that had been unleashed by the Nazis. The world insisted that the Germans accept their guilt. Hence the world denied them the relief of mourning. Their dead lay unburied in their conscience, like Polynices outside the walls of Thebes. As in the *Antigone* of Sophocles, piety called for mourning while politics forbade it.

Exactly what were Strauss's feelings in the matter I do not know. The generally accepted story is that he composed *Metamorphosen* on hearing of the destruction by bombing of the Munich Hoftheater, where so many of his artistic triumphs had been celebrated. The words 'in memoriam' appear in the score at the point where he quotes from the funeral march of Beethoven's Eroica Symphony, and some have interpreted this as indicating that the piece is a memorial to Beethoven.

As with all such speculations, I believe we should step back from the composer's biography and ask ourselves, instead, how *we* might attach a meaning to this great masterpiece. Nielsen and Mitscherlich were fundamentally right, concerning the difficulty that modern Germans find themselves under, when it comes to mourning for their dead. But Strauss's music invites a more general mourning, and one that we too can share. It is contemporary with another work of mourning by a German artist, the extraordinary novel *Dr Faustus* by Thomas Mann. Music is the theme of Mann's novel, which paints the hair-raising portrait of a modern composer who lives under a Faustian pact with the devil, and whose mission is to 'take back the 9th Symphony'. Mann's work too was written in response to the destruction of the German cities. It is a work of despair; but, like Strauss, Mann believed that even in despair, art can bring a message of reconciliation. By showing the spiritual truth of our times, art redeems that truth, incorporates it into the ever-flowing history of consciousness. We can lose everything; but if we are still conscious of that loss and what it means, then there is something that we have not lost. All is not lost, if art remains, to show that all is lost. That is the message of *Dr Faustus*, and for people of my generation this message marked out Mann's novel as the companion piece to Eliot's *Waste Land*: those great works of art were invitations to accept that we live at the end of things, and yet can find cause to rejoice in the fact that we know this, and know what it means.

Strauss's work is a work of music: but it is also *about* music, in something like the way that Mann's novel is about music. Mann's hero tries to remake German music in defiance of itself: his theories (loosely based on those of Schoenberg) involve a rejection of tonality. The idiom of harmony and counterpoint, based on the triad and the scale, is, for Adrian Leverkühn, Mann's composer hero, an exhausted idiom, incapable of capturing the Mephistophelian negation that has now taken up residence in the heart of our civilisation. Tonality must be defied, if music is still to have a meaning. Strauss, by contrast, defies the defiance. In all his late works he tells us that rumours of the death of tonality are exaggerated. We can mourn our lost civilisation in its own musical language.

Metamorphosen is a tribute to the stringed instruments that emancipated Western music from the human voice. Violins, violas and cellos have the inflections of the human voice without the pollution of speech. They are the voice itself, disembodied, transferred to the imaginary space of music and there endowed with a soul. It is the melodic, not the percussive, aspect of the strings that Strauss exploits: none of the instruments plays pizzicato throughout the piece. The work was initially conceived as a string septet. Later Strauss reworked it for twenty-three solo instruments, bringing to the fore its contrapuntal character.

This contrapuntal organisation is telling us something, not about music only, but about the nature of our civilisation in general and Germany's contribution to it in particular. If it is not too pompous a way of putting it, western civilisation is itself a contrapuntal achievement. It arose through the contest and conciliation of many voices, moving freely and independently, but harmonising through law and custom, without the need for any enforced unity or control from above. This fact had been noticed by the philosophers of the Enlightenment, and in particular by Adam Smith in Scotland and Schiller in Germany. Ours is an order arising out of freedom, a form of collective adjustment and conciliation. And it is this that had been jeopardised by the fascist and communist dictatorships of the 20th century, which sought to impose a new and conscripted unity on the people, organised by a single Party under a single command. And, just as regimentation had destroyed the civilising process in Germany, so had it destroyed German music, imposing the artificial order of serialism on what should have been the spontaneous singing of the human voice. In *Metamorphosen* Strauss was celebrating a lost form of social order, with a contrapuntal texture that recalls the 40-part motet *Spem in alium* by Thomas Tallis. Polyphony of this complexity always points the listener in a religious direction. And Strauss's work is no exception. In mourning our civilisation, it tells us, we are also turning towards God. Not that Strauss was a believer: only that he understood the religious need of human beings, and answered to it in his music.

The reference to the stumbling theme of the Eroica slow movement is not the only allusion contained in this piece. The second subject takes off from the lament of King Marke, in *Tristan and Isolde*, over the faithless Tristan. You can read a lot into this. Tristan and Isolde have been taken far beyond the daylight world of social order, into a darkness from which there is eventually no return. Marke is grieving not only over the loss of his friend and his wife, but over the destruction of everything by a force that erupts uncontrollably into human affairs from another region, the region where death and sacrifice are the ruling principles. Yet his grieving leitmotiv has a supremely human tenderness – it contains an offer of forgiveness, of the kind that only a parent can make, and at the same time a recognition that the two lovers lie beyond the reach of forgiveness, in a world where the voice of duty is silenced, and death reigns supreme. Just such a world was Germany at the end of the Second World War.

Those features are worth noting, I think, since they serve to emphasise the very metaphysical character of Strauss's lament. Like Thomas Mann, he is reaching for a kind of *absolute* mourning, one that passes beyond the grief for this or that beloved object, to embrace the loss of everything significant, even the loss of significance itself, as we might put it, the loss of loss. Only this can embrace the enormity of what the Germans had undergone, and the enormity of their own crime in dragging the rest of Europe down with them into the abyss.

For this reason it is impossible to understand this work merely as an elegy. An elegy is a way of accepting the loss of some precious thing. It rejoices in the fact that the precious thing was given. If it is sad, it is with an accepting sadness. An elegy says: this we were given, and it is gone, but we should be grateful for it, and try to live up to its memory. We in England are very familiar with elegiac music. We too suffered loss, but loss of a very different kind, in the First World War, which took away the social order, the pastoral way of life, and the noble aspirations of the English, and dumped us suddenly and brutally in the modern world. Much of our modern music is an invocation of things of which we are bereft. Works like the cello concerto of Elgar, the fifth symphony of Vaughan Williams, and the concerto for double string orchestra of Tippett, invoke our lost pastoral homeland in a spirit of tender regret. They offer us a manageable sadness, which is also an encouragement. Something of all that remains, they say: something to live up to, material to re-forge and recast in a renewed attempt at living rightly. I hear this in the later works of Vaughan Williams, and especially in his *Pilgrim's Progress*. By mourning what we have lost, we also regain it, in another and transmuted form. So the elegy tells us.

I once wrote a book entitled *England: An Elegy*. I was aware when writing it that I was emphasising the good, not the evil, that my country had stood for. But I felt entitled to do so, not merely because the good in my view outweighed the evil, but also because I was embarking on a legitimate work of mourning, just as Elgar had embarked on such a work in his cello concerto. Elegies are attempts at reconciliation and redemption, works of mourning in the sense intended by Freud. Strauss's *Metamorphosen* is not, in that sense an elegy. It is a work *de profundis*, which looks back to what has been lost as the returning traveller looks at the bombed out remnants of his city, in which not a survivor can be found. It is a work without hope, and without any promise for the future. Yet for all that it is a great work of art, and one that still speaks to us.

9

– Dying in Time –

T he old Hippocratic Oath, which enjoins the doctor to aim only to preserve life, belonged to a time when people died young, when infection and injury were the principal causes of death, and when the slow, irreversible decline to which many of us now have to look forward was a rare event, and one that could be accommodated precisely because it was rare. Increasingly, however, doctors and nurses are under pressure to act in ways that will shorten the life of their patients, and this pressure comes both from the patients and from those who love them (not to speak of those who stand to profit by their deaths).

It could be true (and I think it is true) that our moral understanding is rooted in conditions that do not easily make room for such dilemmas. Many of the most pressing 'end of life' issues result from medical advances that have reshaped the human condition, while appealing to moral considerations is appealing to the human condition as it *was*, and not as it is. This does not mean that we have no moral guidance, however. The conscience is ever vigilant, and refuses to go blindly into novel situations. Always it wants an answer, and it wants to reconcile that answer with the intuitions about life and death from which our morality begins. The question is how far, and by what means, those intuitions must be revised in the process.

For example, we have intuitions about justice, and about the relation between justice, which is a right, and charity, which is a privilege, and these intuitions are constantly being challenged, not only by modern medicine but also by the near universal takeover of medical provisions by the state. Maybe it was once the case that doctors and hospitals sold their services to those who could pay for them and gave them free, when they were able, to those who could not. Doctors were then bound by duties of justice to those whom they had contracted to help, and by duties of charity to those who could not afford the contract but who nevertheless had no one else to whom they could turn. The situation was prodigal of dilemmas and irresoluble conflicts; but there is no doubt that the dilemmas and conflicts were radically changed by the appearance of the welfare state, which grants health-care as a civil right to everyone, and makes no distinction between those who can pay for it and those who can't. At once issues of charity and discretion are changed to issues of justice and right. Since resources are scarce there will inevitably be questions of their just allocation. Old people may find themselves then in a weak position, not least because their survival into old age is itself the normal result of universal health-care. The question inevitably arises, whether the state should devote its scarce resources to maintaining a frail old geezer precariously in being, or to treating the ailments and injuries that impair the lives of the young. That is one of many issues in which changes in medical practice and the availability and effectiveness of healthcare have begun to present us with new dilemmas that they do not themselves resolve.

Rather than reflect on the new questions of justice, I wish to consider the changes that have been wrought by modern medicine in our attitude to death. Modern medicine has prolonged the average life-span beyond anything that would have been anticipated a century ago – and naturally there arises the thought that maybe it could, in principle, prolong it forever, offering each of us a medical victory over death itself. About this latter possibility, I have only this to say: that life prolonged by the elixir of immortality would be a life from which the things that we most value – love, adventure, novelty, courage, benevolence, compassion – would inexorably leach away. If you don't believe this, then you should read *The Makropulos Case*, of Karel Čapek, or (better still) listen to the opera that Janáček made from this play.[1]

And besides, by what right do we clutter the planet with our permanent presence, so leaving no room for future generations? If this is where medicine is heading then we have a moral obligation to stop it now.

In contraposition to the fantasy of eternal life on earth I suggest that we have important and useful intuitions concerning the right time to die. Nietzsche made the idea of timely death fundamental to his morality. His own death was preceded by ten years of mental vacancy: about as untimely a death as one could imagine. But his intention was to remind us that what we value in life may be damaged by longevity, and that the achievements and affections that give purpose to our being may be retrospectively eroded by our future decline. This will perhaps seem strange when we consider the matter only from our own point of view. An extra bit of life, even if troubled by aches and regrets, is still a bonus. Hanging on is surely better than falling off, when falling off means ceasing. Thus it is normal to think that

> The weariest, and most loathed earthly life
> That age, ache, penury and imprisonment
> Can lay on nature, is a Paradise
> To what we fear of death.
>   *Measure for Measure*

The point is that there is no retrospective view of my death that is available to me: my death can be known and thought about only in the future tense.[2] Hence there is no way that I can so arrange things in my thinking as to see my death as timely. It occurs for me always in the future, the horizon of my decision-taking. But the judgement of timeliness can be made only from a point beyond that horizon – a point that I cannot reach.

But we don't and can't see things only from our own point of view. I believe that we can make some progress if we put our point of view to one side and adopt the third person perspective. In this perspective we see human life in terms of values and projects that are independent of our own urge to survive. And when we consider things seriously, we are presented with another concept of human life than the one that is familiar to the biologist. We encounter the *moral* concept of human life. Human life, from the moral point of view, is not a special case of the biological category that we know as life in other organisms. We do not understand human life simply as the process whereby a human being endures from birth to death. We understand it as a continuous and developing drama, with a meaning that resides in the whole, and which is not reducible to the felt significance of its parts.

A life is an object of judgment, like a work of art; and judgment means viewing it from *outside*, as the life of another. That, to my mind, is the real definition of the moral point of view. It is the point of view of the other, which sees the self as another too. And the life-concept has its home in the moral point of view. That is why the Greek sages told us to judge no man happy until he is dead. They meant that the worthwhileness of a life is a property of the *whole* life, and that death and dying are as much part of that life as the experiences that precede them. Anybody who has lived through some great affliction, loss or humiliation knows that nothing of our past is really secure. The greatest love, the greatest achievement, the greatest renown can be poisoned by some sudden reversal – as when a woman learns of her husband's infidelity and sees her own love, in which she had deposited her trust and happiness, as wasted, or as when some famous politician, whose corruption has been exposed, reads contempt in all the faces that previously had glowed with admiration.

Thus states of being that seemed at the time to be unquestionably worthwhile, can be retrospectively poisoned, lose their smiling aspect, and come to seem like proofs of weakness. To live to the point where that happens is surely to live too long – for it is to enter a time of regret, like the man who loses a fortune overnight, having not used a penny for his own enjoyment. It is important, therefore, to know what features of the human condition can bring about that sudden change. Ancient wisdom tells us that the reversal of our happiness comes with shame or humiliation – adverse judgement in the eyes of others. To put the point in a more modern idiom: reversal occurs when our life loses its objective support in the 'I-thou' relations that hitherto defined us. Just as 'having a life' is a moral idea, so is 'losing a life'. And the secret of happiness is to die before that loss occurs.

It was therefore perfectly coherent of the ancient Greeks, of the Japanese, of the Romans, of the Anglo-Saxons and of other such warrior people to believe that death is to be preferred to a shameful survival

– so that, for example, battle can present you with a situation in which it is right to die. Plutarch, Livy and others abound in moral stories that turn upon the decision, taken by some ancient hero or heroine, to put an end to a life that would be better, overall, if ended now than if continued into the future. And even when the subject himself is not the agent of his death, and is taken away by some accident or against his will, it is perfectly coherent to think that he might, in this or that circumstance, have died at the right time (before some shame or misfortune that otherwise threatened to engulf him, for instance).

Those ancient ways of thinking reflect circumstances that have to a great extent disappeared – lives that were more precarious, more exposed to external threat, and more lived in the eyes of judgement, than our lives today. But they bring home to us that there is nothing incoherent in believing that a life can be comfortable, healthy and even buoyed by affection, yet have gone on too long – beyond the point at which it would have been right to die. (Cf. the words of Brutus and of Cleopatra's servant Charmion, on taking their own lives, as reported by Plutarch.) If we ever entertain similar thoughts today, it is seldom for the reasons rehearsed by Plutarch and others – seldom because we judge continued life to be shameful, or unworthy of the person we took ourselves to be. Nevertheless, we share with Plutarch's heroes the view that death is not the worst thing that can happen to us.

And our way of thinking, like that of Plutarch's heroes, is imbued with moral ideas. A person lives too long when his or her survival has become a moral offence. This may happen because of something he or she has done: even those who don't believe in the death penalty will admit that a person can so forfeit the privilege of living that his survival is an insult to his victims. Whatever *he* thinks, the rest of us believe that he is living beyond his time. It is perfectly coherent too for people to believe that it is wrong to live to the point where one's life has become a burden, when one has the benefit neither of projects of one's own nor the love of others. This thought arises from another moral perspective than that which propelled Brutus or Cleopatra. It is not the fear of shame and humiliation that is in question, but rather the sense that the value of a life lies to a great extent in the love of those who cherish it. To lose the possibility of that love is to lose what makes life worth living. For the Christian, of course, we can never lose the possibility of another's love. God's love flows perpetually over all of us, and we need only open our hearts to receive it. But it is partly the decline of the Christian vision that has made the question of longevity so urgent for us today.

There is another and more self-centred idea of timely death that feeds into our modern sensibility. This idea is self-directed rather than other-directed. It has both a positive and a negative aspect. In the positive aspect it is the idea of a perfect satiation in the moment, beyond which further life would be a life downhill. The thought is expressed by Keats in his *Ode to a Nightingale*:

> Now more than ever seems it rich to die,
> To cease upon the midnight with no pain . . .

Those lines, written by a doomed poet, speak to all of us. We see life not only as a whole, to be understood as a complete statement, with a beginning and an end. We see it as a succession of moments, and in some precious few of those moments we encounter a concentration of the whole of things, like the sky contained in a drop of dew. Because the moment vanishes, we regret surviving it, since in that instant, we are granted a vision that we can only lose or pollute by swamping it with future experiences.

But this positive aspect of the sensuous idea is counter-balanced by a more frightening negative aspect, which is the suffering that precedes death and which makes death welcome in another way, as the only exit from intolerable pain. Those who commit suicide in order to avoid pain act from a very different motive from those who commit suicide in order to avoid shame. Those who kill themselves from shame are trying to *rescue* their life, by removing the annihilating gaze of the other. Those who are seeking a way out of pain are not trying to rescue their life, but merely to end it. They are not attempting to triumph in the face of defeat; they are not completing a drama that requires just *this* as its ending. They are avoiding pain, no less, no more.

Shame and pain are both invitations to put an end to one's life. But there is another way of out-living life, which is the way of debility and decline. The person whose mind has gone, who can make no decisions for himself, or who has in some way fallen out of human relations is someone whose life is, so to speak, over before its end. The death of a person is not, like the death of an animal, a mere terminus to life. It is the envelope in which a life is contained, and a light that shines along the path that leads to it. At least, that is what we would like it to be, and what it was for Brutus and Cleopatra. But when a person loses his personality before dying, it is as though the envelope of his life is torn. His life seeps messily out of its container, and what might have been complete and worthy becomes instead increasingly disorderly and scattered as the years wear on.

Of course, there are many cases here. But the case I am imagining is one in which the victim loses his capacity to relate to others, and is an object of love only because he is remembered as such, and not because he has the ability to give or receive love now. He has become a burden to his relatives, and also to himself. Yet he is not in such pain that death would be a mercy. Nor is he suffering from some shame or humiliation that would turn his thoughts in that direction – indeed, nothing turns his thoughts in any direction at all.

The worthwhile life is not something that we understand or realise alone. Life becomes worthwhile through relations with others, in which mutual affection and esteem lift our actions from the realm of appetite and endow them with significance – significance for the others who observe them and acknowledge them as worthy, and significance for that very reason for ourselves. The wholeness and fullness of our lives is not revealed to us alone, and is not to be achieved without help: it is a wholeness and fullness that has its origins in the judgement and affection of those whom we encounter. To live beyond the point in which their approval and love can be called upon is to live into a moral wilderness, a place of shadows and negations, compared with which even the Hades of the ancients, as the ghost of Achilles describes it in the *Odyssey*, is a place to be desired. And this wilderness lies before us all, if we live beyond the point where understanding, will and inter-personal relations still govern our conduct.

Now many people will look after a relative who has reached such a state, loving his memory and loving him too on account of it. But others will find it impossible to make the necessary sacrifices, since they will find love turning to toleration, toleration to irritation and irritation to anger or despair. Hence, increasingly, the response to this kind of irreversible decline is to put the victim into a home, where he will be cared for by professionals whose care will be reliable, just and cold. This use of precious resources and precious human capital is hard to justify in utilitarian terms – which I take to be a criticism of utilitarianism, rather than a criticism of institutional care. And it raises in an acute form the question whether we should not do more than we do, collectively and individually, to work for a timely death. Maybe we should be more prepared than we are to take death into our own hands, and not to leave it to an unfathomable fate to settle the question.

Now, modern medicine and healthcare have made it normal to survive into a time of life when our mental capacities and physical competence are in steep decline. We fear this, but we go on taking the medicine and visiting the doctor. The fear is rational, but the medication less so. We are presented with a continuous choice – to wear out the body while we still inhabit it, and then make the best exit we can, or to go on postponing the moment of truth to the point when we are no longer able to do anything to help ourselves. The person who has done so much to stave off death, that he has staved it off to the point where he is unable to make any clear decisions in the face of it, is not someone to whom we *owe* any help, when it comes to deciding what to do.

The question that concerns me, then, is just how we can aim at a timely death, and what would be right or wrong to do in pursuit of it. I find nothing to disapprove of in the suicides of Brutus or Cleopatra, as

Plutarch and (following him) Shakespeare describe them. It would be impertinent, it seems to me, to say that those great human beings had no right to do what they did. But they made it their own responsibility, and in doing so made the act beautiful and generous, an acknowledgement of the wider world and of their duty towards it. What, though, of you and me, creatures who have been maintained in the amniotic bath of the welfare system, who have spent a life avoiding danger and are looking forward to spinning out our pleasures for as long as we can? When should we make such a decision, how and why? And what should others do to help us?

I think we should make a clear distinction here between death conceived as an escape from pain, and death conceived as a protection against mental decline. The first can be understood and acted upon on another's behalf; the second can only be understood and acted upon on behalf of oneself. Thus all who care for the terminally ill, whether professionally or out of love and attachment, wish to alleviate suffering. And if the means of doing so also shortens the patient's life that will be only a secondary concern. I envisage successor drugs to morphine and codeine that will painlessly weaken vital systems, so granting the 'easeful death' that Keats invoked. Of course there will be those furious characters like Dylan Thomas, who will implore their dying dependents not to 'go gentle into that good night', and to 'rage against the dying of the light'. But those who forget their own drama, and attend in love to the one who really matters, will surely agree that the discovery of such drugs, and their use by professionals under proper supervision and control, will do something to justify all those other and more questionable medical advances that have brought us face to face with the horrible diseases of old age. If such drugs exist, then it would surely not be homicide either to ask for them or to administer them – provided only that the diagnosis of terminal illness is secure.

The difficult case is that of mental decline. What should we do – if anything – to escape a future without those distinguishing attributes that make us persons for each other and for ourselves – understanding, self-consciousness, inter-personal emotions, and the ability to face each other 'I' to 'I'? Those capacities are fundamental to personhood, and to lose them is to cease to exist as a person, even while continuing to exist as a human being. Of course, this ceasing to exist as a person does not cancel the right to life or make it any less a crime for another to peremptorily take that life away. The crime here is comparable to that of infanticide. Piety requires us to respect life that was once the life of a person, just as we respect life that one day will become the life of a person.

So the question is this: is there anything that it is permissible for me to do now, by way of putting in place the timely death that will spare me such a fate? Should I, for example, take up some dangerous sport that will ensure that, when the first onset of debility occurs, I make the fatal mistake that leads to my death? But what if the mistake is not fatal, and leads instead to life in a wheelchair? And how can one plan for death prior to debilitation, when it is only in a state of debilitation, when all plans are at an end, that the plan is justified?

From ancient times it has been the role of the philosopher to show us how we should think of death, so as to overcome our fear of it. Epicurus and following him Lucretius argued that there is nothing to fear in death since death is nothing: I do not survive it, so there is nothing bad for me on the other side of it. In an important sense death doesn't happen to me: when I am, death is not; and when death is, I am not. That is just one example of the attempt to neutralise the fear of death by thinking. More recent philosophers have taken the line that it is not thinking but doing that counts. Thus Heidegger tells us that we overcome our anxiety by adopting another existential posture than that of everyday instrumentality. He calls this posture 'being-towards-death', and implies that by adopting it we incorporate death into our lives, overcome its fearful quality, achieve a kind of serenity in action that takes full cognisance of our mortality.

Whatever we think of those arguments they don't help us with the problem of senility. Maybe I don't fully survive the onset of senility; but enough of me survives for it to be true that senility is something that happens to me, and which, in happening, takes away something of supreme value, which is the envelope of my life, the proper death which would have completed me. And as for Heidegger – being-towards-death sounds grand and inspiring as an existential posture. But being-towards-senility has no comparable appeal.

The question is, how should I live now, and what preparations should I make, in the face of this threat – the threat of living beyond my own self-identity as an acting, knowing, loving creature? I think we should take inspiration from Aristotle, and switch the focus of the question. Here, roughly, is the picture that Aristotle paints of the moral life. I cannot know now what will be my future circumstances or desires. All I can know are various general truths about the human condition, and about the dispositions of character that enable people to deal successfully with the contingencies of life. Success in action means acting in such a way that others would admire and endorse you. And happiness comes about when we see our own condition as others might see it, and see also that it is good to be the thing that we are. All I can do now therefore, to confront the vicissitudes of a future life that I cannot predict, is to acquire the dispositions that I would admire in another – the dispositions that we know as the virtues. For Aristotle as for most ancient thinkers these dispositions are clustered around a central core – the four cardinal virtues of prudence, courage, justice and temperance, which between them ensure our moral robustness and our acceptability in the eyes of others. All I can do now to guarantee my future happiness is to exercise the virtues, so that they become part of my character, and so that, when the time comes, I do what is worthy and honourable and earn the approbation of those on whose good opinion I depend. Of course the virtuous person may suffer where the vicious person would not. In battle, for instance, it is often the courageous man who dies, the coward who survives – but survives to what purpose? And in the ordinary business of life the coward is overcome and defeated by the slightest adversity, and is always at one remove from the happiness that he aims for.

Likewise, if we are to confront the threat of senility we should first address the question of the virtues that would enable us to deal with it. And this means the dispositions in another person that would elicit our admiration, and which would show him or her to be in some way victorious in the confrontation, as Brutus snatched victory from defeat when he fell on his sword. One thing that always elicits a negative response in the observer is cowardice. People who cannot bear the thought of death, who have done nothing to understand or accept it, who flee from it or who deceive themselves into thinking that it can be indefinitely postponed elicit in all normal people the thought, let me not be like that! And those who avoid the fear of death by having their bodies frozen, to be revived when medical science is able to give them another go, do not merely repel us with their cowardice: they also exhibit a monstrous selfishness, in refusing to relinquish the planet to their successors, and choosing instead to burden the earth with their unappealing presence for all time. It is just such people who will push medicine in the morally repugnant direction advocated by Aubrey de Grey and the transhumanists – towards the goal of immortality.

Courage therefore is the *sine qua non* of any attempt to deal with the threat of senility – courage to face the truth, and to live fully in the face of it. With courage a person can go about living in another way – a way that will give maximum chance of dying with his faculties intact. This other way is not the way of the welfare culture in which we are all immersed. It does not involve the constant search for comforts or the obsessive pursuit of health. On the contrary, it is a way of benign shabbiness and self-neglect, of risky enjoyments and bold adventures. It involves constant exercise – but not of the body. Rather, exercise of the person, through relationships with others, through sacrifice, through the search for opportunities to be involved and exposed. Such, at least, is my intuition. The life of benign shabbiness is not a life of excess. Of course you should drink, smoke, eat fatty foods – but not to the point of gluttony. The purpose is to weaken the body while strengthening the mind. The risks you take should not damage your will or your relationships, but only your chances of survival. Officious doctors and health fascists will assail you, telling you to correct your diet, to take better forms of exercise, to drink more water and less wine. If you pursue a life of risk-taking and defiance the thought-police will track you down, and your life style will be held up to ridicule and contempt. It is not that anyone intends you to live beyond your time. Rather, to use Adam Smith's famous image, the old people's gulag arises by an invisible hand from a false conception of human life – a conception that does not see death as a part of life, and timely death as the fruit of it.

Each of us must decide for himself what the life of benign shabbiness requires of him. Obviously dangerous pursuits like hunting and mountaineering have a part to play. Equally important is the forthright expression of opinion, so as to win grateful friends and implacable enemies, a process that enhances both the consolations of social life, and the tensions of day-to-day living. I am not sure that I could live like my friend the writer and campaigner Ayaan Hirsi Ali; but there is an adorable recklessness in her truth-directed way of life that makes each moment of it worthwhile. Going out to help others, in ways that involve danger and the threat of disease, is also a useful form of exposure. The main point, it seems to me, is to maintain a life of active risk and affection, while helping the body along the path of decay, remembering always that the value of life does not consist in its length but in its depth.

10

– Conserving Nature –

Environmentalism has all the hall-marks of a left-wing cause: a class of victims (future genera-tions), an enlightened vanguard who fights for them (the eco-warriors), powerful philistines who exploit them (the capitalists), and endless opportunities to express resentment against the successful, the wealthy and the West. The style too is leftist: the environmen-talist is young, dishevelled, socially disreputable, his mind focused on higher things; the opponent is dull, middle aged, smartly dressed and usually American. The cause is designed to recruit the intellectuals, with facts and theories carelessly bandied about, and ac-tivism encouraged. Environmentalism is something you *join*, and for many young people it has the quasi-redemptive and identity-bestowing character of the twentieth-century revolutions. It has its military wing, in Greenpeace and other activist organisations, and also its intense committees, its *odium theologicum* and its campaigning journals. Environmentalists who step out of line like Bjørn Lomborg, author of *The Skept-ical Environmentalist*, are denounced at the important meetings, and thereafter demonised as heretics. In short, it has the appearance of those secular religions, like socialism, communism and anarchism, which turned the world upside down during the 20th century. Hence conservatives are instinctively opposed to it, and begin to look around for facts and theories of their own, in order to fortify their conviction that global warming, loss of biodiversity, rising sea levels, widespread pollution, or whatever, are simply left-wing myths, comparable to the 'crisis of capitalism' prophesied by the 19th-century socialists.

However, the cause of the environment is not, in itself, a left-wing cause at all. It is not about 'liberating' or empowering the victim, but about safeguarding resources. It is not about 'progress' or 'equality' but about conservation and equilibrium. Its following may be young and dishevelled; but that is largely because people in suits have failed to realise where their real interests, and their real values, lie. Environmentalists may seem opposed to capitalism, but – if they understood matters correctly – they would be far more opposed to socialism, with its gargantuan, uncorrectable and state-controlled projects, than to the ethos of free enterprise. Indeed, environmentalism is the quintessential *conservative* cause, the most vivid instance in the world as we know it, of that partnership between the dead, the living and the unborn, which Burke defended as the conservative archetype. Its fundamental aim is not to bring about some radical reordering of society, or the abolition of inherited rights and privileges. It is not, in itself, interested in equality, except

between generations, and its attitude to private property is, or ought to be, positive − for it is only private
ownership that confers *responsibility* for the environment as opposed to the unqualified right to exploit it,
a right whose effect we saw in the ruined landscapes
and poisoned waterways of the former Soviet empire.

But how should conservatives shape their environmental policies? What laws should they pass, and
what resources should they protect? The temptation is
to embrace some comprehensive plan, like Roosevelt's
plan for national parks − to protect some part of the
environment in perpetuity, and meanwhile to control
by law the use of the remainder. However, such statist
solutions go against the grain for conservatives − they
pose a threat not just to individual liberty but also to
the process (of which the free market is the paradigm
instance) whereby consensual solutions *emerge*. State
solutions are imposed from above; they are often without corrective devices, and cannot easily be reversed
on the proof of failure. Their inflexibility goes hand
in hand with their planned and goal-directed nature,
and when they fail, the efforts of the state are directed
not to changing them but to changing people's belief
that they have failed. The ruination of the Dutch and
Danish coastal landscape by banks of hideous wind
turbines is a case in point. They stand in looming
white ranks on every horizon, waving white arms like
disconsolate ghosts, blighting the landscape with their
nightmare vision of judgement day. People put up with

them because they have been told that they are the solution to depleted energy resources. Yet they produce
only a small amount of power, will never be able to
replace the coal-fired power stations that provide the
bulk of the country's electricity, and have all kinds of
negative environmental effects, not least on the populations of migrating birds. However, states don't easily
admit to their mistakes; and the official propaganda
continues to speak as though the wind farms were the
lasting proof of socialist rectitude.

Another and more serious example is observable
in America. The most important man-made environmental problem in this country is that presented by
the spread of the suburbs. Suburbanisation causes
the increasing use of automobiles, and the dispersal
of populations in ways that exponentially increase the
consumption of energy and non-degradable packaging. Conservatives argue that this is a result of freedom and the market. People settle outside the towns
because that is what they want. They are moving out in
search of green fields, wooded gardens, tranquillity –
in short, their own little patch of nature. But this is not
so. They are not moving out in search of a natural environment, but in search of a suburban environment,
and they are doing so because the suburban environment is massively subsidised by the state. The roads,
the infrastructure and the schools – all are state invest-
ments, which entirely imbalance the natural economy
of the town, and make it easier, safer and cheaper to

live on the edge of it – an edge that is constantly moving further from the centre, so destroying the advantages offered to those who move to the suburbs just the year after they move. The mechanism here is not a free market mechanism. Much of the expansion of the suburbs proceeds by the exercise of 'eminent domain' – that provision in American law which gives the official bodies powers of expropriation equal to, and sometimes exceeding, the powers exerted by the socialist governments of Europe. Roads are one obvious instance of this, and the mania for building them in order to maintain traffic flows at a level arbitrarily imposed by official bodies, is the most important cause of the reckless mobility of American society. The true market solution to the problem of traffic congestion – which is to get out of your car and walk – is not, in America, available, since there is no way that you could walk to your destination. Be it the shop, the church, the school or just your nearest friend, suburbanisation has put your goal beyond pedestrian reach.

But you cannot live in the centre of the cities any more, the suits complain: they're not safe. Downtown is for blacks and hispanics; for bums and drop-outs; the schools are appalling, the crime-rate soaring and the place rife with drugs, alcohol and prostitution. Well yes, that's exactly what happens, when the state subsidises the suburbs, imposes zoning laws that prevent proper mixed use in the towns, and engages in its own gargantuan housing projects which drive the middle classes out of the city centers. All this occurs in defiance of the market solution and, as Jane Jacobs pointed out in *The Death and Life of American Cities*, it deprives the city of its eyes and its ears, of its close communities and natural fellowship. Do the Italian cities have crime-ridden centres like the American? Why is it that everyone wants to live in the middle of Paris and not on the edge?

I mention the example not only because it illustrates how far environmental damage has advanced and how difficult it will be to rectify it, but also because it illustrates two rather more important points: first, the mistaken view that it is the market, and not the state, that has created the problem; and secondly the equally mistaken view that the environment can be discussed without raising questions of aesthetics. In my view the problems come precisely when we interrupt the normal ways in which people solve their problems by free interaction. In other words, the problems come from expropriating the paths of rational consensus – as they are expropriated by the state, whenever it uses its powers of eminent domain. And the solutions come when we allow our aesthetic sense to take over, aiming at what looks right, what feels right, and what we can vindicate to the eyes and hearts of our neighbours. American cities have decayed because vast tax-funded resources have been available for the building of roads and housing projects, for the purchase and demolition of otherwise habitable slums, for the horizontal spread of infrastructure, and for the imposition of crazy zoning laws which ensure that where you can buy things you cannot do things, and where you can do things you cannot live. And the solutions to these problems emerge when people, constrained by the natural limitations posed by the need to reach consensual solutions, and without the gargantuan schemes of officialdom, set about building a neighbourhood that looks right to those who live in it, and which is welcoming to those who buy and sell and work.

As I discuss in 'Building to Last', this is something that Leon Krier has illustrated, in his designs for Poundbury on the Prince of Wales's estate in Dorset. As architect in charge he has imposed no overarching plan, no zoning, no publicly owned building, and only those roads that the houses themselves require. He has not set any limit to height but only to the number of stories of the houses, and left people free to build as they choose, provided only that their houses *fit in* with those of their neighbours, using materials and details that conform to a publicly accepted aesthetic, and defining public spaces and streets that are endorsed by the population as spaces and streets of their own. The result is an aesthetic success, and for that very reason an environmental success: compact, sparing in its use of space, with roads that are narrow but not congested since you don't need to drive on them to reach your natural destination, be it shop, pub, friend or school. Energy consumption per head is a fraction of American suburban levels, and crime, in those self-policing streets, is non-existent.

Needless to say, leftists hate Poundbury: so stuffy, so cosy, so much a sign of aristocratic patronage and bourgeois ownership. Its very nature as a consensual solution to the problem of urbanisation, and the absence of a socialist town council with vast amounts to spend on infrastructure, social housing and the well-meaning maintenance of criminals, has made it a symbol of environmental sin. Even the relative absence of automobiles has not saved Poundbury from condemnation. The automobile, an object of leftist contempt and hostility when driven by ordinary bank-managers, is a symbol of emancipation and equality when driven by the real working class. The absence of cars from the streets of Poundbury is therefore read as an absence of the proletariat: the whole thing is just a Christmas-card fantasy of the retired middle classes, and one that bypasses and obscures the need for real and 'sustainable' solutions to the problems of modern housing. It is, in the end, precisely the respect paid to aesthetic values that gets up the leftist nose: only the anti-aesthetic of the modernists and the futurists has any appeal on the left, since only such an aesthetic can be reconciled with the burning desire of leftist movements in every age and clime, which is to tear things down or, failing that, to blow them up.

But look at the solutions that leftists, over the years, have admired, and you will surely learn to distrust their judgement. The great housing projects, inspired by the rhetoric of socialists like Gropius and Meyer or fascists like Le Corbusier, which have invariably involved the clearing of vast areas, and which have themselves had to be demolished within twenty years – what kind of an environmentally friendly solution were they? The crazy idea that power and other facilities should be seen as 'public goods', to be secured by the state on terms dictated by the state – what is this quintessentially leftist idea, if not the root cause of our growing environmental problems? Not only has the 'public good' approach to energy and infrastructure catalyzed the unsustainable spread of populations. It has removed from ordinary people the obligation to think long and hard about their use of energy, and to make the kind of deals with their neighbours that would produce sustainable solutions to real problems. It has made energy into a massive *collective* problem precisely by destroying the sense that it is, for each of us, a real and challenging individual choice.

Here is another example of what I am getting at: light pollution. OK, this is not a major environmental disaster, not yet at least. All it does is consume a lot of energy uselessly, burn away the night sky, disrupt migration patterns and the life-cycles of insects, make it easier for burglars and rapists to find their targets and deprive us of the most beautiful of all natural spectacles and the source of the wonder and tranquillity without which we are less likely to see the point of being alive. Small losses perhaps. But would these losses have occurred if the provision of power, roads, services and utilities had been the responsibility of each pioneer, and not of the government? Once available anywhere, electric light is turned on everywhere, shone with ruthless and half mad exultation into the eyes of God, to make its own contribution to the biological imbalances that we are now encountering.

How should conservatives respond? Hemming in a bit of nature and giving it the status of a national park does something to keep things going. But it is a temporary solution and suffers from all those state-engendered defects that I have just been delineating. The point must always be borne in mind that spoliation occurs for one reason above all others, which is that human beings strive to externalise the cost of everything they do. If they cannot pass on the cost to their neighbours, they will pass it on to future generations. And the most effective instrument ever devised for externalising the cost of individual actions is the state. Its impersonal, administrative and self-justifying nature makes it a perfect vehicle for absorbing the costs of my action now, and depositing them on the unknown others who will one day have to deal with my detritus. In general, therefore, the more the state intrudes into our transactions, the easier it is to escape the cost of them, and the worse the long-term environmental damage. There are exceptions to that rule of thumb, but they should not distract us from its general truth. Nor should they distract us from the complementary truth that the most effective way of ensuring that people internalise their costs is to ensure that they encounter, in fact or in feeling, those upon whom they would otherwise inflict them. Small-scale dealings between neighbours are self-correcting, and the free rider is seldom allowed to get away with it for long. If the people of a village are charged with disposing of their own waste, you can be sure that they will do so in the most ecologically acceptable way. If a state-owned cart comes each week to collect it, then the villagers will be largely indifferent to the fact that it is disposed of in ways that poison some distant waterway.

If we are to find long-term solutions we need to find the motives that keep people in real and reciprocal relation with each other, whether here and now, or across the generations. These motives exist and have been central to conservative thinking, just as they have been absent from thinking on the left. They comprise the two states of mind from which conservatism arose in the 18th century, and which distinguish conservatism from all its phony libertarian and cosmopolitan substitutes: the love of beauty, and the love of home. From Burke and de Maistre to Oakeshott and Kirk, the leading conservative thinkers have devoted much of their thought to the problems of aesthetics, knowing that our search for beauty is not just a matter of private whim, of no lasting concern to the species, but on the contrary, a way in which we strive to shape the world to our needs, and our needs to the world.

Perhaps the most persistent error in aesthetics is that contained in the Latin tag that *de gustibus non est disputandum* – that there is no disputing tastes. On the contrary, tastes are the things that are most vigorously disputed, precisely because this is the one area of human life where dispute is the whole point of it. As Kant argued, in matters of aesthetic judgement we are 'suitors for agreement' with our fellows; we are inviting others to endorse our preferences and also exposing those preferences to criticism. And when we debate the point we do not merely rest our judgement in a bare 'I like it' or 'It looks fine to me'; we search our moral horizons for the considerations that can be brought to judgement's aid. Just consider the debates over modernism in architecture. When Le Corbusier proposed his solution to the problem of Paris, which was to demolish the city and replace it with a park of scattered glass towers and raised walkways, with the proletariat neatly stacked in their boxes and encouraged to take restorative walks from time to time on the trampled grass below, he was expressing a judgement of taste. But he was not just saying, 'I like it that way.' He was telling us that that is how it ought to be: he was conveying a vision of human life and its fulfilment, and proposing the forms that gave the best and most lucid expression to that vision. And it is because the city council of Paris was rightly repelled by that vision, on grounds as much moral and spiritual as purely formal, that Le Corbusier's aesthetic was rejected and Paris saved.

Likewise, when I dispute with my leftist friends about the Dutch and Danish windmills – windmills whose blank and spectral faces are now beginning to stare across my native English woods and fields – we don't just exchange likes and dislikes, as though discussing the rival merits of Cuban and Dominican cigars. We discuss the visual transformation of the countryside, the disruption, as I see it, of a long-established experience of home, and what this means in the life of the farmer, and the presence, as my leftist friends see it, of the real symbols of modern life, which now stand on the horizon of the farmer's world, summoning him to the realities which he has avoided for far too long. By disputing tastes in this way we are not *just* striving for agreement. We are working our way towards a consensual solution to long-term problems of settlement: we are discovering the terms on which we might live side by side in a shared environment, and how that environment should look in order that we can put down roots in it. Conceived in this way aesthetic judgement is the primary form of environmental reasoning: it is the way in which human beings incorporate into their present decisions the long-term environmental impact of what they do.

It has been normal for human beings, down the ages, to find the sight of garbage heaped in the street aesthetically repugnant: hence the standard approach to garbage has been to bury it out of sight – a perfect example of a consensual aesthetic solution that also protects the environment. Likewise the aesthetic revulsion towards litter is the motive from which a consensual solution to non-degradable packaging might one day emerge – for it is a revulsion that already incorporates a long-term vision of the moral and spiritual unseemliness of this kind of waste. And the ecological disaster of the American city stems almost entirely from the fact that – at a certain point – aesthetic principles were abandoned, neighbourhoods were demolished and rebuilt by people who neither lived in them nor looked at them, and building types were adopted on grounds that were never subjected to aesthetic appraisal. The business of building the city was prised free from the constraints contained in aesthetic judgement and surrendered to the utilitarian madness of the bureaucrats.

Leftists are, on the whole, hostile to aesthetic solutions, dismissing them as cosy, comfortable or kitsch. They campaign against the classical revival in architecture as 'pastiche', and against the New Urbanism of people like Krier. They see the countryside conservationist movements as the work of privileged people trying to monopolise the views from their windows. Sometimes their arguments have a point; but their hostility to aesthetic judgement goes deeper than the arguments that occasionally justify it. Consensual solutions, like the old pattern-books of vernacular architecture, which enabled people to slot their houses into a common street, and to build side by side without offending the neighbour, typify the conservative approach to society. These consensual solutions take the form of traditions, conventions, easy-going ways of accepting one's lot and making common cause with one's neighbours. They are quintessentially *unthreatening*, and contain no admonitions of the puritanical kind that appeal to leftists, whose fundamental desire is to *shake people up*, to undermine complacency, and to appear at those tranquil windows like a vision of the apocalypse. The reason why the environmental movement has been captured by the left is that it lends itself to this ambition. It provides terrifying scenarios which seem to justify the total overthrow of existing orders, while encouraging the kind of control from the top that would put enlightened leftists at last in charge of the endarkened middle class. But it could be that the middle class, with its plodding adherence to aesthetic norms, might have had the solution to the environmental problem all along, and that it was only the growth of the modern state, with its arrogant schemes and inability to respond to its own massive failures, that has jeopardised our future.

That brings me to the second important motive from which conservatism arises, which is the love of home. This too is anathema to leftists. All attempts to build the love of home into some kind of political order offend against the cosmopolitan uprootedness of the left intellectual. What is worse, they smack of nationalism, of xenophobia, of those fundamental distinctions between 'us' and 'them' which are the natural effect of settlement and which cause people to do and think the appalling things of which leftists so much disapprove. Thanks to the love of home people defend their country from its internal enemies (McCarthyism); they campaign against illegal immigration (xenophobia); they resist multiculturalism (racism) and insist on bringing up their children in their own ancestral faith (Christian fundamentalism). All the lamentable habits of middle America can be seen as expressions of this single instinct, and all are under attack for that very reason.

Yet it is the love of home that provides the most effective motive on which the environmental movement can call – more effective even than the habit of aesthetic judgement. I think that leftists, over the years, have become aware of the greatest weakness in their philosophy, which is that the ordinary citizen has no motive to go along with it. He may have a grievance against the person who got the job he was aiming for; but that does not make him an advocate of 'social justice'; he may be interested in contributing to sports facilities at the local school, but that does not mean that he wants the state to own the children or dictate what can be taught to them. On the whole his motives are as the conservative supposes them to be: love for his family and his home, and a desire to get along fine with the neighbours. This love of home spreads outwards to include his country, its customs, and its flag; and it is this outreach of the homing instinct that will awaken him, when prompted, to the environmentalist's cause. It is precisely because conservatism, in its political form, is a systematic defence of the nation and its future, that environmentalism is the natural conservative cause.

Many environmentalists on the left will acknowledge that local loyalties and local concerns must be given a proper place in our decision-making, if we are to counter the adverse effects of the global economy. But they will tend to baulk at the suggestion that local loyalty should be seen in national, rather than communitarian, terms. However, there is a very good reason for emphasising nationality. For nations are communities with a political shape. They are predisposed to assert their sovereignty, by translating the common sentiment of belonging into collective decisions and self-imposed laws. Nationality is a form of territorial attachment. But it is also a proto-legislative arrangement. And it is through developing this idea, of a territorial sentiment that contains the seeds of sovereignty within itself, that conservatives make their distinctive contribution to ecological thinking.

Rather than attempt to rectify environmental and social problems on the global level, conservatives seek local controls, and a reassertion of local sovereignty over known and managed environments. This means affirming the right of nations to self-government, and to the adoption of policies that will chime with local loyalties and sentiments of national pride. The attachment to territory and the desire to protect that territory from erosion and waste remain a powerful motive, and one that is presupposed in all demands for sacrifice that issue from the mouths of politicians. For this motive is the simple and powerful one, of love for one's home.

Take the example of Great Britain. Our environment has been a preoccupation of political decision-making for a very long time. Landscape, agriculture and climate have been iconised in our art and literature and become foundational for our sentiments of national identity. Our planning laws, immigration laws and transport strategies until recently reflected this. However, we also know that our country is overcrowded, that its environment is being eroded by urban sprawl, commuter traffic and non-biodegradable waste, that its agriculture is under threat from European edicts and that – largely on account of the recent surge in immigration – our population is growing beyond our capacity to absorb the environmental costs. Sentiments of national loyalty can be called upon to gain support for policies that would control these entropic effects, and which would reflect the long-standing conservative goal, of maintaining an inherited body politic in being, as an autonomous and self-reproducing unit. At this local, national, level, coherent environmental policies and coherent conservative policies seem to me to coincide.

And it is only at this local level that I believe it is realistic to hope for improvement. For there is no evidence that global political institutions have done anything to limit the global entropy – on the contrary, by encouraging communication around the world, and by eroding national sovereignty and legislative barriers, they have fed into that global entropy and weakened the only true sources of resistance to it. I know many environmentalists who seem to agree with me that the WTO is now a threat to the environment, not merely by breaking down self-sufficient and self-reproducing peasant economies, but also by eroding national sovereignty wherever this places an obstacle before the goals of multinational investors. And many seem to agree with me that traditional communities deserve protection from sudden and externally engineered change, not merely for the sake of their sustainable economies, but also because of the values and loyalties that constitute the sum of their social capital. The odd thing is that so few environmentalists follow the logic of this argument to its conclusion, and recognise that we too deserve protection from global entropy; that we too must retain national sovereignty as our greatest political asset in the face of it; and that we too must retain what we can of the loyalties that attach us to our territory, and make of that territory a home. Yet, in so far as we have seen any successful attempts to reverse the tide of ecological destruction, these have issued from national or local schemes, to protect territory recognised as 'ours' – defined, in other words, through some inherited entitlement.

What hope is there that conservative politicians will respond to that argument, and recognise that the environment is *their* cause, and not the cause of their opponents? Among the frail and tentative expressions of political opinion that define the new British Conservative Party some vague and apologetic remarks have been made which, kindly interpreted, might be seen as a provisional endorsement of the environmentalist agenda. In America, however, the GOP remains bullish in its defence of road-building, oil consumption, and grandiose projects. While refusing to subsidise Amtrak or to revive the wonderful railway network, it is subsidising roads and airlines. Instead of setting its face against the energy industry and its great project to suburbanise the continent, it endorses the ever-increasing abuse of the right of eminent domain to send power lines, roads and bridges to every place that has not yet been overrun by the prevailing madness. It has never responded to the arguments of Jane Jacobs in *The Death and Life of Great American Cities*, or those of James Howard Kunstler in *The Geography of Nowhere*; nor has it made any move to endorse a genuine American aesthetic that would give comfort to the New Urbanists and their friends. Its response to the growing problem of non-degradable packaging is total silence, and its leading members seem to be entirely happy with an economy that imports millions of tons of plastic every week from China in exchange for America's only genuinely degradable product, which is the dollar.

Who should we blame for this? Some point their finger at the free marketeers, saying that their philosophy is one that endorses big business, whatever big business might do. But that, I think, would be a mistake. The free market, as defended by Mises and Hayek, is simply an instance of the kind of consensual problem-solving that I have been advocating in this article. The Burkean argument for a partnership across generations is an argument of the same kind, which asks us to recognise that consensual solutions may sometimes require that we consult the interests of the unborn and the dead. What has gone wrong, it seems to me, is not the attachment of conservatives to the market, but the failure to see what a real market solution requires: namely the retreat of the state and its projects from every decision in which local aims and loyalties are at stake. It is surely time for conservative politicians to recognise that, with really big issues, you need to think small.

11

– Defending the West –

I don't think we will understand the confrontation between the West and radical Islam if we do not recognise the enormous *cultural* shift that has occurred in Europe and America since the ending of the Vietnam war. The citizens of Western states have lost the appetite for foreign wars; they have lost the hope of scoring any but temporary victories; and they have lost confidence in their way of life, and indeed are no longer sure what that way of life requires of them.

At the same time their people have been confronting a new opponent, who believes that the Western way of life is profoundly flawed, and perhaps even an offence against God. In a 'fit of absence of mind' Western societies have allowed this opponent to gather in their midst, sometimes, as in France, Britain and the Netherlands, in ghettoes which bear only tenuous and largely antagonistic relations to the surrounding political order. And in both America and Europe there has been a growing desire for appeasement: a habit of public contrition, an acceptance, though with heavy heart, of the censorious edicts of the mullahs, and a further escalation in the official repudiation of our cultural and religious inheritance. Twenty years ago it would have been inconceivable that an Archbishop of Canterbury should give a public lecture advocating the incorporation of *shari'ah* law into the legal system of England. Today many people consider this to be an arguable point, and perhaps the next step on the way to peaceful compromise.

All this suggests to me that we in the West will go through a dangerous period of appeasement, in which the legitimate claims of our own culture and inheritance will be ignored or downplayed, in the attempt to prove our peaceful intentions. It will be some time before the truth will be allowed to play its all-important role, of rectifying our current mistakes, and preparing the way for the next one. This means that it is more than ever necessary for us to rehearse the truth, to come to a clear and objective understanding of what is at issue. I will therefore spell out some of the critical features of the Western inheritance, which should be understood and also defended in the current confrontation. Each of these features marks a point of contrast, possibly of conflict, with the traditional Islamic vision of society. And each has played a vital part in creating the modern world. Islamist belligerence stems from finding no secure place in that world, and turning for refuge to precepts and values that are at odds with the Western way of life. This does not mean that we should renounce or repudiate the distinguishing features of our civilisation, as many would have us do. It means that we should be alert in their defence.

The first of the features that I have in mind is citizenship. The consensus among Western people is that the law is made legitimate by the consent of those who must obey it. This consent is delivered by a political process through which each person participates in the making and enacting of the law. The right and duty of participation is what we mean by 'citizenship', and the distinction between political and religious communities can be summed up in the view that political communities are composed of citizens, religious communities of subjects – of those who have 'submitted' (which is the primary meaning of the word *islām*). And if we want a simple definition of the West as it is today, it would be wise to take the concept of citizenship as our starting point. That is what the millions of migrants are roaming the world in search of: an order that confers security and freedom in exchange for consent.

Traditional Islamic society sees law as a system of commands and recommendations laid down by God. These edicts cannot be amended, though their application in particular cases may involve jurisprudential argument. Law, as Islam has seen it, is a demand for our obedience. And its author is God. In a certain measure that is the opposite of the conception of law that we have inherited with the idea of citizenship. Law for us is a guarantee of our freedoms. It is not made by God but by man, following the instinct for justice that is inherent in the human condition. It is not a system of divine commands, but a residue of human agreements.

This is particularly evident to British and American citizens, who have enjoyed the inestimable benefit of the common law – a system which has not been laid down by some sovereign power, but on the contrary built up by the courts, in their attempts to do justice in individual conflicts. Our law is a 'bottom up' system, which addresses the sovereign in the same tone of voice that it uses to address the citizen – namely, by insisting that justice, not power, will prevail. Hence it has been evident since the Middle Ages that the law, even if it depends on the sovereign to impose it, can also depose the sovereign if he tries to defy it.

As our law has developed it has permitted the privatisation of religion, and of large areas of morality. To us it is not just absurd but oppressive that there should be a law punishing adultery. We disapprove of adultery; but we also think that it is none of the law's business to punish sin just because it is sin. In the *shari'ah*, however, there is no distinction between morality and law: both stem from God, to be imposed by the religious authorities, in obedience to God's revealed will. To some extent the harshness of this is mitigated by the tradition which allows recommendations as well as obligations as rulings of the Holy Law. Nevertheless, there is still no scope in the *shari'ah* for the privatisation of the moral, still less of the religious, aspects of life.

Of course, most Muslims do not live under

shari'ah law: only here and there, in Saudi Arabia and Afghanistan, for example, is the attempt made to impose it. Elsewhere Western codes of civil and criminal law have been adopted, following a tradition begun in the early 19th century by the Ottomans. But this recognition accorded to Western civilisation by the Islamic states has its dangers: for it inevitably provokes the thought that the law of the secular powers is not really law; that it has no real authority, even that it is a kind of blasphemy, as Sayyid Qutb, former leader of the Muslim Brotherhood, argues in his seminal work *Milestones.* Rebellion against the secular powers is easy to justify, when their law is seen as usurping the sovereign authority of God.

From its origins therefore, Islam has found it difficult to accept that we stand in need of any other law, or any other sovereign, than those revealed in the Koran; hence the great schism which divided Shi'ite from Sunnite over the matter of the legitimate succession. From the point of view of secular government, questions of legitimate succession are settled by the very same constitution that governs the daily operation of the law: ultimately they are a matter of human agreement. But a community that believes itself to be governed by God, on terms conveyed by his messenger, has a real problem when the messenger dies: who takes over, and how? The fact that rulers in Islamic communities have a greater than average tendency to end up assassinated is not unconnected with this

question. The Sultans of Istanbul surrounded themselves with a household guard of Janissaries chosen
from their Christian subjects, precisely because they
could not trust any Muslim to ignore the opportunity
of rectifying the insult to God contained in the person
of a merely human ruler. The Koran itself speaks to the
point, in 3, 64, addressing Jews and Christians with the
command to take no divinity beside the one God and
no lords (*ārbābān*) from among each other.

Citizenship and secular law go hand in hand.
We are all participants in the process of law-making:
hence we can view each other as free citizens, whose
rights must be respected, and whose private life is their
own concern. And it is this that has made possible the
privatisation of religion in Western societies and the
development of political orders in which the duties
of the citizen take precedence over religious scruples.
How this is possible is a deep and difficult question
of political theory; *that* it is possible is a fact to which
Western civilisation bears incontrovertible witness.

But that brings me to the second feature which I
identify as central to European civilisation, which is
nationality. No political order can achieve stability if it
cannot call upon a shared loyalty, a 'first-person plural'
that distinguishes those who share the benefits and
burdens of citizenship, from those who are outside the
fold. In times of war the need for this is self-evident;
but it is as necessary in times of peace, if people are
really to treat their citizenship as defining their public

obligations. National loyalty marginalises loyalties of family, tribe and faith, and places before the citizen's eyes, as the focus of his patriotic feeling, not a person or a group but a country. This country is defined by a territory, and by the history, culture and law that have made that territory *ours*. Nationality is composed of land, together with the narrative of its possession.

It is this form of territorial loyalty that has enabled people in Western democracies to exist side by side, respecting each other's rights as citizens, despite radical differences in faith, and without any bonds of family, kinship or long-term local custom to sustain the solidarity between them. National loyalty is not known everywhere in the world. And it is not known in the places where Islamists are rooted. Consider Somalia. People sometimes refer to Somalia as a 'failed state', since it has no central government capable of making decisions on behalf of the people as a whole, or of imposing any kind of legal order. But the real trouble with Somalia is that it is a failed nation. It has never developed the kind of secular, territorial and law-minded loyalty that makes it possible for a country to shape itself as a nation state rather than an assembly of competing tribes and families.

The same is true of many other places where Islamists are bred: even if they do function as states, like Pakistan, they are often failures as nations. They have not succeeded in generating the kind of territorial loyalty which enables people of different faiths, different kinship networks, different tribes to live peacefully side by side, and also to fight side by side on behalf of their common homeland. And their recent history might lead us to wonder whether there is not, in the end, a deep conflict between Islamic conceptions of community and the conceptions which have fed our own idea of national government. Maybe the nation state is an anti-Islamic idea.

This observation is, of course, pertinent to the Middle East today, where we find the remnants of a great Islamic Empire divided into nation states. With a few exceptions this division is the result of boundaries drawn on the map by Western powers, and notably by Britain and France as a result of the Sykes-Picot accords of 1917. It is hardly surprising if Iraq, for example, has had such a chequered history as a nation state, given that it has been only spasmodically a state, and never a nation. It may be that Kurds, Sunnite Arabs and Shi'ites in Iraq could all come, in time, to see themselves as Iraqis. But this identity will be fragile and fissiparous, and in any conflict the three groups would identify themselves in opposition to each other. Indeed, it is only the Kurds who seem to have a developed *national* identity, and it is an identity opposed to that of the state in which they are included. As for the Shi'ites, their primary loyalty is religious, and they look to the homeland of Shi'ism in Iran as a model in turbulent times. Hence, in the current conflict with the Islamic State, it is the Iraqi Shi'ites, together with their Iranian and Lebanese co-religionists, who are in the front line of the fighting.

Not all the nation states carved out of the Ottoman Empire are as arbitrary as Iraq. Turkey, which saved itself as the rump of the Empire, succeeded in recreating itself as a genuine nation state – though not without the expulsion or massacre of non-Turkish minorities. Lebanon and Egypt had enjoyed a kind of quasi-national identity under Western protection from the mid 19th century. And of course Israel has established a thoroughly Western form of national government, over territory which is disputed for that very reason. But the examples in no way serve to allay the suspicion that Islam is not friendly to the idea of national loyalties, and certainly not friendly to the idea that, in a crisis, it is national rather than spiritual allegiance that should prevail.

Consider Turkey. Atatürk created the Turkish nation-state by imposing a secularist constitution, adopting a secular legal system based on French and Belgian models, outlawing Islamic dress, expelling the *'ulema'* from public office, forbidding polygamy, rooting out Arabic words from Turkish and adopting the Latin alphabet, so cutting off the language from its cultural antecedents. The conflict between the secular state and Islam was thereby pushed underground, and for a long time it seemed as though a stable compromise had been achieved. Now, however, the conflict is erupting all over again. There has been an attempt by secularists to outlaw the ruling Islamic Party, recent electoral victors in a landslide vote, and also an attempt by the government to arraign leading secularists in a terrorist trial of dubious legality.

Lebanon owes its exceptional status to its erstwhile Christian majority, and to the long-standing alliance of Maronite and Druze against the Ottoman Sultan; its current fragility is largely due to Hezbollah, which allies itself with Iran and Syria and rejects Lebanon as a national entity to which its loyalty is owed. Egypt has survived as a nation state only through radical measures taken against the Muslim Brotherhood, and only by leaning upon a legal and political inheritance which would probably be rejected by the Muslim population (though not by the Copts) in any free vote. As for Israel, it has been condemned by its neighbours to live in a permanent state of siege.

This leads me to the third central feature of Western civilisation: Christianity. I have no doubt that it is the long centuries of Christian dominance in Europe which laid the foundations of national loyalty, as a loyalty above those of faith and family, and on which a secular jurisdiction and an order of citizenship can be founded. It may sound paradoxical, to identify a religion as the major force behind the development of secular government. But we should remember the peculiar circumstances in which Christianity entered the world. The Jews were a closed community, bound in a tight web of religious legalisms, but governed from

Rome by a law which made no reference to any God and which offered an ideal of citizenship to which every free subject of the Empire might aspire.

Christ found himself in conflict with the legalism of his fellow Jews, and in broad sympathy with the idea of secular government – hence his famous words in the parable of the Tribute Money: render unto Caesar what is Caesar's and to God what is God's. The Christian faith was shaped by St Paul for the use of communities within the Empire, who wanted only space to pursue their worship, and had no intention of challenging the secular powers. And this idea of dual loyalty continued after Constantine, being endorsed by Pope Gelasius the First in the 6th century, in his doctrine of the two swords given to mankind for their government, that which guards the body politic, and that which guards the individual soul. It is this deep endorsement of secular law by the early Church that was responsible for the subsequent developments in Europe – through the Reformation and the Enlightenment to the purely territorial law that prevails in the West today.

During the early centuries of Islam the philosophers attempted to develop a theory of the perfect state. But always religion was at the heart of it; Al-Fārābī even tried to adapt the argument of Plato's *Republic*, with the Prophet as philosopher-King. When finally all discussion stopped, at the time of Ibn Taymiyya in the 14th century of our era, it was clear that Islam had turned its back on secular government, and would henceforth be unable to develop anything remotely like a national, as opposed to a religious, form of allegiance. The most important advocate of Arab nationalism in recent times, Michel Aflaq, was not a Muslim but a Greek Orthodox, born in Syria, educated in France, and dying in Iraq disillusioned with the Ba'ath party that he had helped to found. If national loyalties have emerged in recent times it is in spite of Islam and not because of it. And they seem peculiarly fragile and fissiparous, as we have noticed in the case of Palestinian attempts at national cohesion, and in the chequered history of Pakistan.

Christianity is sometimes described as a synthesis of Jewish metaphysics with Greek ideas of political freedom. And no doubt there is truth in this – which is hardly surprising, given the historical context of its inception. And it is perhaps the Greek input that is responsible for the fourth of the central features that I believe worthy of emphasis, when addressing the confrontation with Islam, and that is irony. There is already a developing streak of irony in the Hebrew Bible, one that is amplified by the Talmud. But there is a new kind of irony in Christ's judgements and parables, which look on the spectacle of human folly and wryly show us how to live with it. A telling example of this is Christ's verdict in the case of the woman taken in adultery: 'Let he who is without fault cast the first stone', in other words: 'Come off it; haven't you wanted to do what she did, and already done it in your hearts?'

It has been suggested that this story is a later inser-
tion – one of the many culled by the early Christians
from the store of inherited wisdom attributed after his
death to the Redeemer. Even if that is true, however,
it merely confirms the view that the Christian religion
has made irony central to its message. This irony is
shared by the great Sufi poets, and especially by Rumi
and Hafiz. But it seems to be largely unknown in the
versions of Islam that shape the souls of the Islamists:
theirs is a religion which refuses to see itself from outside, and which cannot bear to be criticised, still less
to be laughed at – something we have abundantly witnessed in recent times.

Indeed this is nowhere more apparent than in the
matter that called forth Christ's ironical judgement.
Not only is stoning to death still officially endorsed
in many parts of the Muslim world as a punishment
for adultery; in many Islamic communities women are
treated as prostitutes just as soon as they step out of
the line drawn for them by men. The subject of sex,
which cannot be usefully discussed without a measure
of irony, has therefore become a painful topic among
Muslims, confronted as they inevitably are by the lax
morals and libidinous confusion of Western societies.
Our mullahs are unable to think about women as
sexual beings, and unable to think for very long about
anything else. As a result an enormous tension has developed in the Muslim communities in Western cities,
the young men enjoying the surrounding freedoms,

the young women hidden away and often terrorised lest they should do the same.

Irony was seen by the late Richard Rorty as a state of mind intimately connected with the postmodern worldview – a withdrawal from judgement that nevertheless aims at a kind of consensus, a shared agreement not to judge.[1] It seems to me, however, that irony, although it infects our states of mind, is better understood as a virtue – a disposition aimed at a kind of practical fulfilment and moral success. If I were to venture a definition of this virtue, I would describe it as a habit of acknowledging the otherness of everything, including oneself. However convinced you are of the rightness of your actions and the truth of your views, look on them as the actions and the views of someone else, and rephrase them accordingly. So defined, irony is quite distinct from sarcasm: it is a mode of acceptance, rather than a mode of rejection. And it points both ways: through irony I learn to accept both the other on whom I turn my gaze, and also myself, the one who is gazing. Irony is not free from judgement: it simply recognises that the one who judges is also judged, and judged by himself.

And this brings me to the fifth notable feature of Western civilisation that is at stake in the current confrontation: the feature of self-criticism. It is second nature to us, whenever we affirm something, to allow a voice to the opponent. The adversarial method of deliberation is endorsed by our law, by our forms of education, and by the political systems that we have built to broker our interests and resolve our conflicts. Think of those vociferous critics of Western civilisation such as the late Edward Saïd and the ubiquitous Noam Chomsky. Saïd, for example, spoke out in uncompromising and at times even venomous terms on behalf of the Islamic world against the residual outlook, as he saw it, of Western imperialism. So what happened to him? He was rewarded with a prestigious chair in a leading university, and with countless opportunities for public speaking in America and around the Western world: just as Chomsky has been. This habit of rewarding our critics is, I think, unique to Western civilisation, and the only shame is that, in American universities, things have gone so far that there are no rewards for anyone else. The prizes are distributed on the left, because this feeds the ruling illusion, that self-criticism will bring us safety, and that all threats come from ourselves and from our desire to defend what we have.

There is another critical feature of Western civilisation which grows from the habit of self-criticism, and that is representation. We in the West, and the English-speaking peoples pre-eminently, are heirs to a longstanding habit of free association, in which we join together in clubs, businesses, pressure groups, and educational foundations. This associative genius was particularly remarked upon by de Tocqueville in his journeys through America, and it is facilitated by the unique branch of the English common law – equity and the law of trusts – which enables people to set up funds in common and to administer them without asking permission from any higher authority.

This associative habit goes with the tradition of representation. When we form a club or a society that has a public profile we are in the habit of appointing officers to represent it. The decisions of these officers are then assumed to be binding on all members, and cannot be rejected without leaving the club. In this way a single individual might be able to speak for a group, and in doing so bind them to accept the decisions made in their name. We find nothing strange in this, and it has affected political, educational, economic and leisure institutions in our society, in incalculable ways that it would be otiose to spell out. It has also affected the government of our religious institutions, both Catholic and Protestant. Indeed, it was among 19th century protestant theologians that the theory of the corporation as a moral idea was first fully developed. We know that the hierarchy of our church, be it Baptist, Episcopalian or Catholic, is empowered to take decisions on our behalf, and can enter into dialogue with institutions in other parts of the world, in order to secure the space that we require for our worship.

Association takes a very different form in traditional Islamic societies. Clubs and societies of strangers are rare, and the primary social unit is not the free association but the family. Companies did not enjoy a developed legal framework under Islamic law, and it has been argued by Malise Ruthven and others that the concept of the corporate person has no equivalent in that law.[2] Charities are organised in a completely different way – not as property held in trust for beneficiaries, but as property that has been 'stopped' (*waqf*); and all public entities, such as schools and hospitals, are regarded as ancillary to the mosque and governed by religious principles. Meanwhile the mosque itself is not a corporate person, nor is there an entity which we could call the Mosque, on the analogy of the Church – an entity whose decisions are binding on its members, which can negotiate on their behalf, and which can be held to account for its misdeeds and abuses.

As a result of this long tradition of associating only under the aegis of the mosque or the family, Islamic communities lack the conception of the spokesman.[3] When there are serious conflicts between Muslim minorities and the surrounding society in our cities we have found it difficult, if not impossible, to negotiate, since there is no one who will speak for the Muslim faction or take responsibility for imposing any decision. If, by any chance, someone does step forward, then the individual members of the Muslim community feel free to accept or reject his decisions at will. And the same problem has been witnessed in Afghanistan, Pakistan and other places with radicalised Muslim populations. When someone *does* step forward to speak for some dissident group it is very often on his own initiative, and without any procedure that validates his office. And as like as not, should he agree to some solution, he will be assassinated, or at any rate disowned, by the radical members of the group for whom he purports to be speaking.

This leads me to reflect again on the idea of citizenship. One important reason for the stability and peacefulness of societies based on citizenship is that individuals exist in those societies fully protected by their rights – fenced off from their neighbours in their spheres of private sovereignty, where they alone make the decisions. This means that a society of citizens can establish good relations and a shared allegiance among strangers. You don't have to know your fellow citizen in order to ascertain your rights against him or your duties towards him, and his being a stranger in no way alters the fact that you are each prepared to die for the territory that contains you and the law which you enjoy. This remarkable feature of citizen-states is sustained by the things to which I have referred: by self-criticism, representation and corporate life, and it is not to be observed in traditional Islamic societies. What the Islamist movements promise to their adherents is not citizenship but *brotherhood – ikhwān –* an altogether warmer, closer and more metaphysically satisfying thing.

However, the warmer and closer an attachment, the less widely can it be spread. Brotherhood is selective and exclusive; it cannot be spread very far without exposing itself to sudden and violent refutation. Hence the Arab proverb, I and my brother against my cousin, I and my cousin against the world. The association of brothers is not a new entity, a corporation, which can negotiate for its members. It remains essentially plural – and indeed *ikhwān* is simply the plural of *akh*, brother, and used to denote the assembly of like-minded people brought together by their common commitment, rather than any institution that can claim sovereignty over them. This has significant political repercussions. When Nasser's successor as president of Egypt, Anwar Sadat, set aside seats in the Egyptian Parliament for the Muslim brotherhood, they were immediately occupied by those judged suitable by the president, and disowned by the *real* brotherhood, which continued its violent activities, until contriving the assassination of Sadat. Brothers don't take orders: they act together as a family, until they quarrel and fight.

This last contrast between Western and traditional Islamic communities brings me to a final and critical point of difference. We live in a society of strangers, who associate rapidly and tolerate each other's differences. Ours is not a society of vigilant conformity; it makes few public demands that are not contained in the secular law; and it allows people to move quickly from one group to the next, one relationship to the next, one business, religion or way of life to the next. It is endlessly creative in finding the institutions and associations that will enable people to live with their differences and to remain on peaceful terms, without the need for intimacy, brotherhood or tribal loyalties. I don't say that this is a good thing; but it is the way things are, and the inevitable by-product of citizenship as I have described it. So what makes it possible to live in this way? There is a simple answer, and that is drink. That which the Koran promises in paradise but forbids here below is the necessary lubricant of the Western dynamo. You see this clearly in America, where cocktail parties immediately break the ice between strangers, and set every large gathering in motion, stimulating a collective desire for rapid agreement, among people who a moment before did not know one another from Adam. This way of quickly coming to the point depends on many aspects of our culture besides drink: but drink is critical, and those who have studied the phenomenon are largely persuaded that, for all the cost that our civilisation has paid in terms of alcoholism, accidents and broken homes, it is thanks to drink that we have been, in the long run, so successful. Of course, Islamic societies have their own ways of creating fleeting associations – the hookah, the coffee house, and the traditional bath-house, praised by Lady Mary Wortley Montague as establishing a solidarity among women that has no equivalent in the Christian world. But these forms of association are also forms of *withdrawal*, a standing back from the business of government in a posture of peaceful resignation. Drink has the opposite effect – bringing strangers together in a state of controlled aggression, able and willing to engage in any business that should arise from the current conversation.

The features that I have referred to do not merely explain the uniqueness of Western civilisation: they also account for its success in negotiating the enormous changes that have come about through technological and scientific advance, just as they explain the political stability and democratic ethos of its component nations. The features also distinguish Western civilisation from the Islamic communities in which the terrorists are bred. And they explain the great resentment of those terrorists, who cannot match, from their own moral and religious resources, the easy competence towards the modern world that we witness in Europe and America.

If this is so, then how should we defend the West from Islamist terrorism? I shall suggest a brief answer to that question. First we should be clear about what it is that we are defending. We are not defending our wealth or our territory, since these are not in issue. We are defending our political and cultural inheritance – and these are embodied in the seven features which I have singled out for attention. Secondly, we should be clear that you don't overcome resentment by feeling guilty, or by conceding your fault. Weakness provokes, since it alerts your enemy to the possibility of destroying you. We should be prepared to affirm what we have and to express our determination to hold on to it. That said, we must recognise that it is not envy, but resentment, that animates the terrorist. Envy is the desire to possess what the other has; resentment is the desire to destroy it. How do you deal with resentment? This is the great question that so few leaders of mankind have been able to answer. But Christians are fortunate in being heirs to the one great attempt to answer it, which was that of Christ, drawing on a long-standing Jewish tradition that goes back to the Torah, and which was also expressed in similar terms by Christ's contemporary, Rabbi Hillel. You overcome resentment, Christ told us, by forgiving it. To reach out in a spirit of forgiveness is not to accuse yourself; it is to make a gift to the other. And it is just here, it seems to me, that we have taken the wrong turn in recent decades. The illusion that we are to blame, that we must confess our faults and join our cause to that of the enemy, exposes us to a more determined hatred. The truth is that we are not to blame, that the enemy's hatred is entirely unjustified, that his implacable enmity cannot be defused by our breast-beating. And this truth makes it seem as though we are powerless.

However, we are not powerless. There are two resources on which we can call in our defence, one public, one private. In the public sphere we can set out to protect the good things that we have inherited. And that means making no concessions to those who wish us to exchange citizenship for subjecthood, nationality for religious conformity, secular law for *shari'ah*, the Judeo-Christian inheritance for Islam, irony for solemnity, self-criticism for dogmatism, representation for submission, and cheerful drinking for censorious abstinence. We should treat with scorn all those who demand these changes and invite them to live where their preferred form of political order is already installed. And we must respond to their violence with whatever force is required to contain it, if we can.

In the private sphere, however, Christians should follow the path laid down for us by Christ, and that means looking soberly and in a spirit of forgiveness on the hurts that we receive, and showing, by our example, that these hurts achieve nothing save to discredit the one who inflicts them. This is the hard part of the task – hard to perform, hard to endorse and hard to recommend to others.

– Notes –

LOVING ANIMALS

1 Michael Woods, Robbie A. McDonald and Stephen Harries, 'Predation of Wild Animals by Domestic Cats in Great Britain', report to The Mammal Society, most recent revision 1 March 2003, available online.

2 Adapting the celebrated remarks on anger in *Nicomachean Ethics*, Book 4, chapter 5.

3 Among the many affecting accounts of this relationship in the literature I single out George Pitcher, *The Dogs Who Came To Stay*, New York, 1995, since I knew the dogs, and know the author.

4 See the important essay by Stanley Cavell, 'The Avoidance of Love: A Reading of *King Lear*', in *Must We Mean What We Say?*, updated edition, Cambridge, CUP, 2002.

5 See *Animal Rights and Wrongs*, London, Continuum, 2002.

GOVERNING RIGHTLY

1 See the reports by Lunacek, Estrella and Zuber, Members of the European Parliament, which you can find presented and analysed on the site of European Dignity Watch: europeandignitywatch.org

2 See Larry Siedentop, *Inventing the Individual: The Origins of Western Liberalism*, London, 2014.

3 See Philip Bobbitt, *The Shield of Achilles*: *War, Peace and the Course of History*, New York, Knopf, 2002.

DYING IN TIME

1 See Bernard Williams's classic essay, '*The Makropulos Case*: Reflections on the Tedium of Immortality', in *Problems of the Self*, Cambridge, CUP, 1973.
2 See the discussion by Vladimir Jankélévitch, *La mort*, Paris, Grasset, 1966.

DEFENDING THE WEST

1 Richard Rorty, *Contingency, Irony, Solidarity*
2 Malise Ruthven, *Islam in the World*.
3 There is an important exception to this rule in the world-wide Ismaʿīlī community, which has found its representative and spokesman in the Aga Khan.

Denial: The Unspeakable Truth
Keith Kahn-Harris

The holocaust never happened. The planet isn't warming.
Vaccines harm children. Denialism comes in many forms, often
dressed in the garb of research. It's insidious and pernicious,
but what if, as Kahn-Harris asks, it actually cloaks much darker,
unspeakable desires? This book sets out to expose what really
lies beneath the denier's arguments.

Questions of Travel: William Morris in Iceland
Lavinia Greenlaw

The Victorian artist William Morris was fascinated by Iceland,
which inspired him to write one of the masterpieces of travel
literature. In a new and composite work, Poet Lavinia Greenlaw
combines excerpts from his Icelandic writings with her own
response to the country.

Happy Half-Hours: Selected Writings of A. A. Milne
Introduced by Frank Cottrell-Boyce

Milne had a talent for turning out a thousand whimsical words
on lost hats and umbrellas, golf, married life, cheap cigars, and
any amount of life's little difficulties. This anthology features
the very best of A. A. Milne in one delightful volume.

*All titles are available in the UK, and some titles are available
in the rest of the world. For more information please visit www.
nottinghilleditions.com

A selection of our titles is distributed in the US and Canada by
New York Review Books. For more information on available
titles please visit www.nyrb.com